£2

B

Digging Up Antiques

Digging Up
ANTIQUES

Edward Fletcher

Pitman Publishing

First published 1975
Sir Isaac Pitman and Sons Ltd
Pitman House, Parker Street, Kingsway, London WC2B 5PB
PO Box 46038, Banda Street, Nairobi, Kenya

Pitman Publishing Pty Ltd
Pitman House, 158 Bouverie Street, Carlton,
Victoria 3053, Australia

Pitman Publishing Corporation
6 East 43rd Street, New York, NY 10017, USA

Sir Isaac Pitman (Canada) Ltd
495 Wellington Street West, Toronto 135, Canada

The Copp Clark Publishing Company
517 Wellington Street West, Toronto 135, Canada

ISBN 0 273 00494 8

Computer Typesetting by Print Origination, Bootle,
Merseyside, L20 6NS.

G10:13

Printed in Great Britain by Unwin Brothers Limited
The Gresham Press, Old Woking, Surrey, England.
A member of the Staples Printing Group

Contents

Introduction

The antiques which lie beneath the soil of Britain do not include Hepplewhite chairs, French mahogany chests or undiscovered Rembrandts, though I do not doubt that one or two old masters and some fine pieces of Georgian furniture lie at this moment gathering dust in unexplored lofts, cellars and garden sheds throughout the land. They will probably be discovered when someone decides to be extra thorough during Spring cleaning and their finding will rate a column or two in your morning newspaper.

Here we are concerned with less spectacular collectors' items which any reader can confidently expect to find by doing a little historical detective work and making use of a few simple tools. The antiques we are seeking are in the main those glass, ceramic and metal objects which our grandparents, great-grandparents and earlier ancestors lost or threw away when their usefulness came to an end—sealed wine bottles, lids from pots which once held cosmetics and foods, heads and limbs from dolls which little girls played with a century ago, military badges from regiments long disbanded, antique weapons, Victorian buttons, clay tobacco pipes and numerous other valuable objects which now lie beneath our mid-20th century feet. They have survived in the ground because they were made from durable materials; they are worth finding because they are the very objects which today grace the displays at antique markets in our cities and towns. The throw-aways of yester-year have become today's prized collectables.

That they can be found by anyone prepared to seek them is confirmed by the photographs in this book which show a selection of objects recovered by British amateur treasure hunters—weekend enthusiasts who find pleasure, relaxation and antiques by digging into Victorian rubbish dumps, 'mudlarking' along riverside foreshores, beachcombing around our coasts and searching old houses about to come under the demolition contractor's hammer. The number of adventurous spirits actively engaged in bottle collecting, relic hunting and similar activities runs to several thousands. There are amateur treasure hunting and bottle collecting clubs in most counties where members co-operate on research, recovery and the compiling of records on finds made. One of Europe's largest glass container manufacturing companies sponsors the British Bottle Collectors' Club and an annual prize is awarded for the best bottle found. In addition the various branches of amateur treasure hunting have their own magazines which are widely read by all connected with the hobby.

Thousands of finds have been made during the few years in which the popularity of amateur treasure hunting has grown to its present level, but readers as yet uninitiated into the secrets of where and how to find their own antiques in the ground may take heart from my assurance that many more similar 'treasures' await the diligent searcher. The following chapters on where and how to find likely hunting grounds and the information which accompanies the illustrations in the book should soon put any determined treasure hunter on the track of his or her first buried antique. May I wish such readers success in the hunt!

Acknowledgements

The author and publishers are grateful to the following who have supplied some of the photographs which illustrate this book: Radio Times Hulton Picture Library, pp. 2, 3 and 5; The Scottish Tourist Office, p. 6; Dan Cruickshank, p. 22.

1 Victorian rubbish dumps

Collection and disposal of rubbish

Many antiques recovered from beneath the ground have come from 19th-century rubbish dumps which contain an enormous variety of bottles, pot lids, earthenware, clay tobacco pipes, dolls' heads and other collectors' items. Armed with digging tools and some knowledge of how and where Victorians disposed of their household refuse it is possible to build an impressive collection by recovering the objects they threw away.

Throughout the Victorian era organized collection and disposal of rubbish on a large scale was limited to cities and towns. In rural areas those who lived in country houses, farms and isolated cottages made their own arrangements for the disposal of unwanted junk, usually by tipping it on a piece of waste ground at the back of the house. Many villages had a communal refuse cart into which each household threw its rubbish. This cart would make one or two trips every week to a convenient hole in the ground which might have been a dried-out pond, a pit from which chalk had been dug to make lime for agricultural use or any site on which crops could not be grown.

Such dumps, although small in size, are worth finding because they hold some of the best examples of early Victoriana. Unlike city refuse, the material which went into the village cart was unsorted. There was not enough of it to make worthwhile the job of hunting through the cart to extract those objects which might have had a re-sale value; everything in the cart went into the dump.

In Victorian cities and towns the economics of refuse collection and disposal were more complicated. It cost money to provide the hundreds of horse-drawn carts and handbarrows needed to collect refuse in large cities such as London, Bristol,

Victorian dump-digging is probably the only hobby which combines antique collecting with keeping fit.

1

Leeds and Glasgow. We pay for our service today with a percentage of our rates but in the first half of the 19th century all city and town corporations obtained the funds necessary to provide the service by selling the contents of their citizens' dustbins to the highest bidder.

An 1870s dust cart.

Cartloads of rubbish collected every day by the city's dustmen were taken to storage areas in various parts of the city. In London the main centre was at Lett's Wharf near Blackfriars Bridge, a site to which hundreds of thousands of tons of household refuse were brought every year. Here, as at every other centre, each cartload was carefully searched by men, women and children known as scavengers. These unfortunate souls were paid a few coppers to sort the contents of the carts. They hunted through the vast mess, waist deep in garbage, to remove every item which could be sold—leather from old book covers, woollen rags, feathers, scrap metal, unbroken bottles, even cinders and the dust from road sweepings—all were valuable. There were leather, rag, feather, scrap metal and bottle merchants eager to buy, and most corporations made handsome profits on rubbish. Bottles were sold to breweries and bottling

2

A London dust yard in 1873.

works, dust and coal ash went to brickmakers and broken
pottery and glass were sold to civil engineering contractors who
found a use for them in roadmaking schemes. The small amount
of unsaleable material was usually burned at the collection centre
and the remains hauled off by barge or railway truck to
outlying marshes.

Fortunately for today's dump diggers this method of paying
for household refuse collection proved uneconomical during the
latter part of the 19th century. By the late 1860s the
ever-increasing amount of rubbish which was collected every
year began to overload the system. Scavengers' wages were cut
and more carts employed; but demand for second-hand bottles,

3

rags, feathers and other recovered materials was beginning to decline as improved manufacturing techniques reduced costs in glass, wool and other industries. A depression in brickmaking also greatly reduced demand for the vast amounts of coal ash which Victorian cities produced.

Faced with these revenue losses most corporations abandoned scavenging as a method of raising money to pay for the collection service. Some were still able to sell unsorted rubbish to brickmakers who burned and screened it at the brickworks to extract useful ash; but by the 1880s there were few corporations which did not have to pay to have their town and city refuse removed by private contractors.

Farmers who owned low-lying, marshy land now found that they could make a handsome profit by leasing dumping rights. Vast areas of Essex and Kent were reclaimed in this way during the late 19th century when London boroughs outbid each other for the rights to dump refuse. Any accessible hole in the ground could provide its owner with a steady income until it was filled. Most favoured sites were those which flanked canals because carriage charges were considerably lower when the refuse could be transported to the site by barge. It was fortunate that many canals had clay pits along their banks from which clay had been extracted to 'puddle' the canal during construction by lining it with impervious clay to prevent water seepage. Now these same holes provided convenient dumping grounds for much Victorian urban refuse.

The railways also shared in the rubbish disposal boom of the late Victorian period. If a site could not be reached by barge a railway company would often lay a track from one of the central refuse collecting points to the dumping ground. In London a track was laid to connect Lett's Wharf with dumps at Meopham and Longfields in Kent. Between 1879 and 1882 some 168,000 tons of London refuse were carried along this line in railway waggons.

'The Procession of Father Thames', a cartoon c. 1858.

4

A likely hunting ground in northern Scotland.

By the turn of the century one or two far-sighted town and city corporations were beginning to realize that the long-term answer to the problem of rubbish disposal was not to be found in seeking an ever-decreasing number of holes in the ground. Soon the first incineration plants were being installed and the days of the scavenger, the horse-drawn cart and the vast fleets of refuse barges began to draw to a close.

It is interesting to note that the coal ash which our late Victorian city fathers found so difficult to get rid of is now in short supply thanks to the sharp decline in the use of coal for home heating and as fuel for power stations. In many towns and cities the old dumps are being excavated to recover Victorian fire grate ash which is urgently needed for 20th-century road-making projects. The wheel has turned a full circle.

Where the dumps are
Having outlined the history of 19th-century refuse disposal methods let us now look briefly at some of the sites on which Victorian dumps are likely to be found throughout the country.

In northern Scotland the majority of the 19th-century dumps are associated with the sites of abandoned crofts. They are small, but rarely contaminated by modern rubbish. Memories are long in the Highlands and it is often possible to learn the exact location of a dump from an old crofter who has spent a lifetime in the district. One method of disposing of refuse in mountainous regions was to tip it into ravines, such sites being especially favoured as village and small town dumps in this part of Britain.

In central Scotland town dumps were often sited in abandoned quarries and mines. Dumping of rubbish into lochs also

5

seems to have been common practice in this region. Around Glasgow and Edinburgh much Victorian refuse was carted to brick-fields and gravel pits.

In northern England and along the Scottish border there are many abandoned farm cottages and mining hamlets where old dumps can always be found. On the east coast Victorian refuse was often tipped over sea cliffs and into 'denes', which are narrow wooded valleys running down to the sea.

The industrial regions of Lancashire, Yorkshire and Durham have numerous 19th-century dumps in abandoned brick-yards, clay and gravel pits, quarries and mines. Unlike many of the old dumps on similar sites further south, most Victorian dumps in northern England are still accessible, untouched by the land shortage which has caused numerous dumps around London to disappear beneath office blocks and motorways.

In Staffordshire old pottery workings hold vast amounts of Victorian refuse, while the numerous canal routes of the Midlands provide some of the best hunting grounds for clay pit dumps. In Northamptonshire Victorian brick-fields absorbed refuse from many towns and cities; further east the marshes of East Anglia provided vast land reclamation sites.

London refuse was carried to all parts of south-east England. It was not uncommon for barges loaded with Victorian rubbish to make round trips of over one hundred miles to carry their cargoes to the creeks and estuaries of Suffolk, Essex and Kent. They also made long journeys upstream to Berkshire and Oxfordshire to dump rubbish into abandoned gravel pits. Clay pits along the banks of every canal flowing into the Thames were filled with the city's refuse and in Essex vast areas of marshland were reclaimed to provide sites for industrial growth. The huge Ford Motor Company complex at Dagenham rests on Victorian London refuse. In Kent the brick-fields and creeks around the Medway estuary provided convenient dumping grounds for both London and Kentish rubbish.

In the agricultural counties of southern England the best sites are those village dumps which have escaped the 20th-century house-building boom. In the cities of Portsmouth and Southampton salt marshes around harbour mouths were used as dumping grounds; in the Bournemouth and Swanage areas 'denes' are again found to have been common Victorian refuse sites.

In the west country and in Wales quarries, abandoned mines, derelict farmhouses and isolated village sites similar to those of northern Scotland are the best hunting grounds for 19th-century dumps.

Local research
In many towns it is possible to pin-point the location of refuse dumps used during the late Victorian period by consulting

6

19th-century records. Public libraries, town or city archives and the offices of borough council refuse disposal departments often keep copies of old minutes and reports which give the exact locations of dumps used by the town before 1900. A search for such documentary information should always be your starting point when attempting to locate an old town dump. Even if the 19th-century records have been lost or destroyed you will be able to eliminate many 20th-century sites by a careful check on more recent documents which can be consulted at such places. Obtain an Ordnance Survey map of the district and mark on it the locations of all post-Victorian dumps. Their positions might indicate likely hunting grounds for earlier sites; if a town dumped its refuse on low-lying marshes or in worked-out quarries thirty years ago it is quite probable that similar sites were used when organized collection and disposal first started.

Geographical clues to the whereabouts of possible sites can also be gleaned by comparing Ordnance Survey maps drawn a hundred years ago with modern maps of the same area. Clay and chalk pits which appear on early maps but which are not now shown are quite likely to have been filled with refuse; changes in the level of land alongside riverbanks can also indicate earlier dumping; and the sites of brickworks which ceased manufacture sixty or more years ago might also be shown on the early map. All such sites should be marked on your modern map as worthy of close inspection.

In cities and larger towns, where hundreds of thousands of tons of refuse were disposed of every year between 1860 and 1900, many dumps would have been used and it is most unlikely that the exact location of each site will be recorded in old city and borough records. Often the minutes merely report the appointment of a certain private contractor who undertook to dispose of refuse for a number of years at an agreed figure per ton. In such cases other lines of enquiry must be followed. A check on Victorian trades directories at the local library might reveal that this contractor owned a fleet of barges or horse-drawn waggons. The contractor, or his successors, could still be in business today and a polite letter to the company secretary often produces evidence of where the company's old dumping grounds were sited. On more than one occasion where I have followed up such a report I have been put in touch with a retired employee who actually worked for a Victorian contractor. Needless to say, such men are mines of information.

Whatever line of enquiry you follow when checking written information on early dumps you must eventually confirm your findings by visiting the sites. Often a physical search of marshes, old quarries, riverbanks and canal sides is the only method of locating a site which can be used because old records no longer exist. It is a search method I wholeheartedly recommend; if carried out thoroughly it *must* lead to the finding of a worthwhile site.

Many newcomers to Victorian dump-digging miss excellent sites because they neglect to search areas of countryside which cannot conveniently be reached by car. The only sites you are likely to find if you refuse to venture more than a few hundred yards from your parked vehicle are those which have already been found by many other bottle or relic hunters, or those on which 20th-century rubbish has also been dumped. The best sites lie well off the beaten tracks—on silted creeks and along the backwaters of river estuaries, on lonely marshes, in deserted quarries and alongside derelict canals. There are few roads to get you there and a boat would probably run aground. The only solution is to sling your digging tools across your back and reach the site on two legs. The reward for such effort is likely to be a choice site into which no other digger has put a fork.

Recently a fellow dump-digging enthusiast and I carried out an experiment to show which method of locating a Victorian dump—research or a physical check of a likely area of countryside—gave quickest results. My friend spent a day browsing in a city's archives; I put a pack on my back and spent the day tramping overgrown towpaths along a derelict canal. As arranged we met that evening in a local pub and when my friend saw me enter through the door of the public bar he blurted out the name of the site on which I had carried out a trial dig that afternoon. I nodded my agreement with his findings and held up a choice pot lid dug from the site a couple of hours earlier.

On another occasion we heard from fellow members of the British Bottle Collectors' Club that an area of land lying between two tidal river estuaries which suggested itself as ideal Victorian refuse disposal country had failed to produce any evidence of dumping during careful research into its recorded 19th-century history. We made a physical check of the area, during which we walked more than forty miles in one day, and discovered three unrecorded dumps which were eventually shown to date from 1880.

Clues on the ground

The most successful Victorian dump-hunters have taught themselves to 'read the ground': to look for those clues which experience has shown to be good indicators of the presence of antiques beneath their feet. Take time to consider the problems which anyone dumping rubbish in a particular area would face and· the effects dumping would have on the surrounding landscape and the clues to look for will be obvious.

If refuse was transported to a site by barge it would be necessary to have off-loading facilities on the canal bank close to the dump. Such facilities might have included mooring points, a crane and barrows or carts to carry the rubbish from the barges to the dump. A generation later most of this equipment will have long since disappeared, but often a few timbers or a derelict cart can be spotted on the canal bank to provide the vital clue to the dump's exact location.

If rubbish was carried to the site in horse-drawn carts traces of the old tracks leading to the dump might still be visible. When they are completely overgrown their directions can often be followed by looking for gaps in fences or for strongly constructed bridges over streams and ditches which suggest that carts must have passed that way at some time.

The ashes and vegetable wastes which were originally thrown into dumps eventually provided a rich fertilizer for weeds. The effects of this are best seen in areas where the natural soil is poor and on which only stunted vegetation normally grows. If you come across a patch of ground thick with lush nettles in such an area it is most likely that the nettlebeds cover an old dump. Elders, which thrive on dry sites, often grow on rubbish dumps and their presence in damp woodland can pin-point a Victorian dump which might otherwise be very hard to find.

Burrowing animals, especially rabbits, love to colonize old dumps. When the natural earth is of a clayey nature rabbits will always make their homes in a dump which is much easier to burrow into. The spoil they throw out can also be profitably checked for pieces of pottery, clay tobacco pipe stem and glass

A scene of desolation on a back-water canal. Such locations are excellent sites on which to seek canal-side dumps.

which will confirm the presence of a site very quickly. Slow worms and lizards also thrive on rubbish dumps; on warm days it is not uncommon to find a lizard basking inside a Victorian bottle which a rabbit has thrown to the surface of the site.

Where former marshland was reclaimed by dumping 19th-century rubbish the land is often used for agriculture if it escapes industrial development. Check such areas in wintertime after the land has been ploughed and you may see large amounts of glass and pottery fragments in the soil; a sure sign that a Victorian dump lies beneath the site.

Village dumps and those associated with isolated houses and farms can usually be located by following overgrown lanes leading from buildings to likely sites. These lanes are just sufficiently wide to have been used by a horse-drawn cart and most of them take a downhill route to the dump to avoid tiring man or beast in getting the loaded cart to the site.

Summary

Area	Possible sites	Clues to dump
Highland regions	Ravines, quarries, mines	Cart tracks leading from buildings — lush vegetation (esp. nettles and elders) — local people
Coastal regions	Cliffs, denes	Cart tracks leading to site
Lowland regions	Marshland	Creeks formerly navigable by barges — mooring and off-loading points
Lowland regions	Former marshland used for agriculture	Glass and pottery fragments on ploughed fields
Industrial regions	Mines, quarries, clay pits, brickfields, canals	Lush vegetation — burrowing animals — cart tracks — derelict equipment on canals — Victorian sites being excavated to recover coal ash

Digging the site

You need only three tools to dig a Victorian rubbish dump—a garden fork, a long-handled shovel and a probe rod, which is a metal rod used to confirm the presence of glass beneath the surface of the ground by pushing it into the suspected dump until you feel the end strike glass. The main things to remember when digging are to ensure that loose material removed to reach the collectable objects is not thrown onto an undug part of the dump and to dig the site methodically so that all objects of value are removed.

The probe rod is used to define the perimeters of the site; a trench is cut along one side and the loosened earth thrown outside the perimeter line. This trench must be sufficiently wide to enable you to use the fork and shovel correctly and, whenever possible, it should be as deep as the dump itself. If the dump is more than six feet deep the depth of your trench must be determined by your own height and strength. Never go so deep that you cannot comfortably throw the loose spoil out of the trench. When you have dug a trench to the required depth along one side of the site and you have extracted all collectable objects you can begin to scrape the walls of the trench with your fork to search the remainder of the dump. Shovel the loosened material behind you as you work and proceed across the site by this 'backfilling' method.

It requires experience to dig a site correctly and at the same time to find all or most of the valuable objects in the dump while keeping breakages to a minimum. I urge you to gain your digging experience by joining a local bottle collectors' club and by taking part in digs on club sites. As I have mentioned, there is a branch of the British Bottle Collectors' Club in almost every county in Britain and there are smaller clubs in many cities and towns. Newcomers to the hobby who may not have succeeded in finding their own sites can gain useful experience from other club members.

As you are sure to be told when you join a local club, you must *never* dig on a Victorian rubbish dump unless you have the landowner's permission to do so. Club secretaries will have already obtained the necessary permission to dig those sites on which the local club is working; but if you prefer to find your own site bear in mind that the land on which you find it, however derelict it may appear, is owned by someone. Do not dig unless that person has agreed to let you do so.

2 Riversides and riverbeds

A king's ransom awaits the fortune hunter who perfects a method of extracting those riches which lie between the low water mark and the dredged channel on every tidal river which has a city or town along its banks. The Thames, the Seine, the Rhine, the Tiber, the tidal rivers of Asia, South America and many countries whose recorded histories are brief in comparison to ours are storehouses of historic relics which lie almost untouched by collectors, historians, archaeologists or treasure hunters.

In Britain there are more than two hundred tidal rivers which certainly hold enormous quantities of coins, jewellery, tokens, badges, medals and other valuable objects lost or thrown into them during the past two thousand and more years. Visit any museum in a city or town sited on a tidal river and read the cards which accompany exhibits of coins, jewellery and other metal objects displayed there. They will confirm that rivers do indeed flow over fortunes.

The most spectacular collection of river-found riches exhibited in this country is to be seen in the British Museum where treasures on display include the Battersea Shield, a superb Celtic helmet and a huge bronze head of the emperor Hadrian—all river finds. The London Museum also has thousands of coins, ornaments and other valuable objects from the Thames; Bristol Museum displays large numbers of relics from the Severn; Newcastle Museum has a rich display of Roman coins from the Tyne; while other notable finds which have been recovered from British rivers include a chest containing twenty thousand silver pennies, a complete ship more than five hundred years old and a diamond-encrusted scabbard from a sword reputed to have been owned by Lord Nelson.

12

Mudlarks

People have been finding valuable objects on riverside foreshores for thousands of years, but it was in Queen Victoria's reign that 'mudlarking'—the scavenging of tidal estuaries for saleable relics—became a full-time occupation for hundreds of men, women and children in cities including London, Bristol, York, Newcastle and Edinburgh. The Thames' mudlarks satisfied demand from Victorian London's professional and amateur antiquarians for Roman and medieval relics. They tramped the muddy foreshores of the river at each low tide and picked up tens of thousands of valuables every year—Celtic coinage, Roman silverware, Anglo-Saxon pottery, Viking weapons and similar finds from every period of our history. Queues of eager buyers would gather at steps and alleyways leading down to the riverside to jostle and haggle for the finds of the day. An Anglo-Saxon coin would fetch a few coppers; a Roman dagger might change hands for a shilling; a bronze statuette for a florin or two. Few mudlarks grew rich by their labours, in spite of the fact that had it not been for their efforts many of our museums would be considerably poorer in 'priceless' exhibits today. They were cheated and robbed at every turn by dealers, collectors and archaeologists who grew rich and famous thanks to the efforts of men, women and children whose names are long forgotten.

Only two are remembered today, not for their finds, but for the way in which they turned the tables on those cheating dealers and collectors. William Monk and Charles Eaton spent twenty years scratching a bare living from the Thames mud and combing the foreshores between Blackfriars and London Bridge for any saleable objects they could find. They were expert mudlarks and included among their regular customers many leading Victorian archaeologists.

On a particularly low tide in 1857 Monk and Eaton were working their favourite stretch of mud on the Southwark foreshore when they spotted a handful of crude lead badges which the falling tide had exposed. The two mudlarks were half inclined to leave the grubby pieces of grey metal where they lay in the mud; they were more interested in a rich harvest of Roman silver coins which the river had been reluctantly giving up for several days past and they spent some time fruitlessly searching for coins before deciding to put the lead badges into their collecting bag. Returning to the City they showed the day's takings to a group of dealers and were surprised when the lead discs were snapped up at a couple of shillings each. The dealers explained to the mudlarks, who were unschooled and illiterate, that their finds were medieval pilgrims' badges and that any more they recovered from the Thames mud would be equally welcome.

A few hours later Monk and Eaton were discussing the day's

events over pints of ale at a local tavern. It seemed unfair to them that a Roman silver coin should fetch no more than a grubby piece of lead. Those dealers had been cheating them for years; here, it seemed, was a fine opportunity to repay them. They took what remained of the day's profits, purchased an ingot of lead from one of the City's metal merchants and hurried home. Working far into the night they fashioned from memory a dozen copies of the relics they had found on the foreshore that day. When the lead cooled they placed the newly cast badges in a bucket of sand and gravel and shook them vigorously for several minutes to scratch and roughen their surfaces. The following day when they produced their 'finds' the dealers fell over themselves to buy and the first 'Billies and Charlies' were on the market.

Three years and several thousand Billies and Charlies later, the Society of Antiquities exposed the fraud, causing many red faces in archaeological circles. As for Billie Monk and Charlie Eaton, notoriety merely served to boost demand for their fakes. No collection of medieval relics was considered complete without a specimen from their workshop and they continued to prosper until 1870 when Charlie died. Today their fake pilgrims' badges change hands at more than £10 each.

Dredgermen

Victorian mudlarks confined their relic-hunting activities to the mud, silt and gravel exposed on riverside foreshores by falling tides. Meanwhile, in deeper waters, another group were hard at work—the dredgermen who kept the navigable channels open to river traffic.

Dredging has been carried on with varying success on many British rivers since medieval times. Towns such as Chester on the Dee, Lewes on the Sussex Ouse, Bawtry on the Idle and York on the Yorkshire Ouse lost the battle with river silt and declined as ports for large vessels many years ago. London, Bristol, Harwich, Hull, Liverpool and others continue the never-ending battle by constantly scouring the main channels to which all vessels must keep when entering and leaving port. The first large-scale dredging operations on the Thames and other important rivers were carried out in the 19th century when engine-powered dredges made it possible to clear the acres of silt, a task which had hitherto been hopeless. In London these operations brought to light thousands of relics from the past which dredgermen, like the mudlarks, sold to collectors and dealers for 'beer money'.

One collector known to every Victorian dredgerman who worked the Thames between Richmond and Wandsworth was Thomas Layton of Brentford. He had a reputation for paying slightly higher rates for river-found relics than his contemporaries and when dredging operations began in the tidal reaches above the City it was to Layton that most of the relics from the silt were first brought.

There were few educated Victorians who were not smitten by the collecting bug; the possession of a 'collecting cabinet' for one's Roman and medieval antiquities was the hallmark of gentility and learning. But Layton was no run-of-the-mill collector. Not content with a mere cabinet, he stacked his entire house and several garden sheds with relics purchased from Thames dredgermen. Occasionally he would lend a few of his purchases for an exhibition, but the bulk of his collection remained hidden away until after his death in 1911. When the chests in his garden sheds were inspected by archaeologists they were found to contain thousands of relics from the river. One chest containing objects dredged up during operations at Brentford contained twenty-eight Middle Bronze Age rapiers, thirty-three Late Bronze Age swords and thirty-four spearheads!

Equally spectacular evidence to show that tidal river silt holds great riches came to light in 1831 when work began on dismantling the old London Bridge which had been replaced by a new structure 150 feet upstream. Silt had built up for centuries around the old foundations and when the first few bucketfuls were dredged up the workmen spotted hundreds of bronze, silver and gold Roman coins. Other objects quickly followed: brass medallions, iron spears, tools, brooches, rings, pottery and a number of bronze statuettes of Mercury, Apollo, Jupiter and Harpocrates. Most of these finds were bought by Charles Roach-Smith, another famous Victorian antiquarian, who eventually sold his entire collection to the British Museum.

By the end of the 19th century most of the navigable channels on Britain's major rivers had been cut. Much of the new dredging work since then has been limited to excavations for concrete embankments and dock expansion schemes. All such projects have brought to light more treasures from our rivers but most of the dredging which goes on today is limited to maintaining existing channels, and it seems unlikely that future dredging for navigational purposes will produce spectacular finds to equal those made in the Victorian era because the silt beds which contain most of the unfound relics and antiquities lie above the sites on which modern dredgers work.

The techniques

What, then, are the prospects for today's antique and relic hunter who tries his luck on tidal riversides? Alas, he cannot hope to equal the success of 19th-century mudlarks who could pick up dozens of valuable objects every day by patrolling the exposed mud and gravel and by keeping their eyes to the ground. Pickings are much leaner nowadays; but, as with all antique and relic hunting, patience pays. It is still possible to acquire a fine collection of riverside relics by diligent search.

John Webb, probably the world's most consistently successful riverside relic hunter.

Select as your first site any tidal foreshore which flows through a city or town with a long and eventful history. The more bridges, moorings, docking areas and riverside streets there are the better will be your chances of good finds. If the foreshore exposed by the falling tide is made up of mud, gravel and large amounts of 20th-century junk in the form of rusty nails, bicycle frames and tin cans, there are certain to be equal amounts of 'junk' from previous centuries. When you get down to the foreshore do not expect to pick up coins, jewellery and other valuables immediately. The average newcomer to mudlarking spends several days finding nothing more exciting than rusty washers. But this unprofitable apprenticeship is the only way to train your eyes to spot the treasures which lurk amongst the riverside junk. You will have successfully completed that apprenticeship when you can distinguish the subtle differences in colour between a rusty washer and a valuable coin camouflaged by river silt. There is no short cut to acquiring that skill.

Recovering relics which lie in the silt below low water mark is a more complicated operation. At the time of writing (July, 1973) no completely satisfactory method has been found, though many attempts at recovery have been made and some have had limited success. Simply stated the problem is this: how

16

can small objects—usually of non-ferrous metal—which lie on a riverbed covered by mud one inch to several feet thick, which is permanently under water one inch to several feet deep, be recovered in sufficient quantities to make that recovery a worthwhile proposition?

A method which works reasonably well when the mud is only a few inches thick is to use a rake with a weighted head to ensure that it cuts sufficiently deep into the bed. The rake must have a long handle and the tines must be 4 or 5 in. long and not more than ½ in. apart. When a strip of wire netting is woven between the tines this tool will trap very small coins and similar objects.

Another method often used by 20th-century mudlarks is to construct a sieve which has three meshes—1½ in., 1 in. and ½ in.—through which mud and gravel extracted from the river with a tool similar to the rake described above is washed. Sophisticated sieves have a motor-driven pump; simple models rely on buckets of water poured onto the top mesh.

Diving equipment is also employed by relic hunters working below the low water mark but so far two major problems have prevented divers finding substantial amounts of river treasure. The first is pollution which inhibits diving on some of the best sites which lie in rivers flowing through industrial cities and towns. It is a problem which is diminishing as river cleansing schemes reduce the amounts of toxic materials which were until quite recently discharged into most British rivers. Ten years from now this problem could be completely overcome.

The second problem which divers face when they descend into muddy rivers is that of extremely poor visibility. If a diver can see four inches in front of his face mask under such conditions he considers himself fortunate. In many cases, and always on the best sites, he must work in near total darkness and rely on his sense of touch to locate objects in the silt. Small wonder that only a handful of divers have achieved significant success when working in tidal rivers!

Miniature dredges which do on a very small scale what a dredging vessel does in the navigable channel have also been used by a few relic hunters. They work on a suction principle and draw to the surface mud and gravel from the riverbed which can then be sieved to extract valuable finds. Suction tubes vary in diameter from 1 in. to 6 in. and the largest models can process quite substantial amounts of material. Their disadvantages include high cost and poor reliability caused by frequent blockages in the suction tube which occur whenever large stones and similar debris are sucked into the nozzle. If costs and blockages could be substantially reduced these machines might have a future in river treasure hunting.

Gold can be successfully extracted from river and stream gravels by the use of riffle boards. If several shovelfuls of river

A suction dredge with riffle board in operation.

gravel containing one or two pin-head size nuggets of gold are washed along a trough having ridges or riffles on its surface the particles of gold will become trapped in the riffles while larger gravel and pebbles are washed away. This principle has been used by prospectors the world over to find alluvial gold in mountain streams and rivers. It works equally well when employed to extract coins, jewellery and other metal objects from river mud. If the material brought to the surface by a small suction dredge is washed over a riffle board all small, non-ferrous objects—coins, rings, badges, brooches, tokens, brass pins, lead weights and similar relics—can be quickly and efficiently extracted.

I stated at the beginning of this chapter that all tidal rivers hold countless valuable and historic relics which lie waiting for those who develop the methods to recover them. Many can already be found by using the principles outlined above, and it seems likely that a complete answer to the problem might be found by combining two or more of these methods—possibly by employing a diver to direct the nozzle of a suction dredge equipped with a riffle board.

Metal detectors

The best relic-hunting sites on riversides are littered with iron nails, brass screws, copper washers, odd pieces of lead and similar objects of little interest to amateur treasure hunters. The valuable finds—coins, jewellery and so on—are intermingled with this foreshore rubbish, and the two must be sorted by sieving, by careful observation, or with a riffle board. Simple and inexpensive metal detectors are incapable of differentiating between the valuables and the junk and are therefore unsuitable for work on many of the best riverside sites.

However, in recent years, more sophisticated metal detectors able to distinguish ferrous from non-ferrous metals have been developed. Used intelligently, these machines can aid the riverside treasure hunter; but I stress the need for careful use. No electronic device will tell you the difference between a valuable medieval lead seal lying six inches under the foreshore mud and a piece of scrap lead from a 20th-century car battery buried at a similar depth. The sophisticated machine will tell you a piece of non-ferrous metal lies beneath its search head, but *you* must dig up the object to decide whether or not it is worth keeping.

If a detector capable of differentiating ferrous and non-ferrous metals is used in conjunction with a plastic sieve it greatly reduces the amount of time normally spent on sieving. Load the plastic sieve with material dug out of the foreshore, then pass the head of the detector over this material. If the metal detector signals the presence of non-ferrous metal the contents of the sieve can be washed through the mesh until the object is found. If no non-ferrous indication is given by the detector the sieve's contents can be discarded without further scrutiny.

Some rivers worth a visit

This list is not comprehensive. Your own local river is likely to hold equally exciting finds.

The Severn. One of our most important navigable rivers from early times, the Severn with its tributaries the Wye and the Warwickshire Avon was, for more than a thousand years, the great highway for all trade and traffic from the entire west country and large areas of the Midlands, Wales and north-west England. The Severn itself was naturally navigable for a distance of 155 miles to Welshpool in Montgomeryshire, and was, until the coming of river improvements and canals, the longest navigable waterway in the country. The city of Bristol, which stands at its mouth, was a great international seaport when Liverpool was still an insignificant fishing village.

The Ouse. While the Severn and its tributaries served the west coast, a group of rivers flowing into the Wash were of equal importance to east coast trade. Of these the Bedford Ouse was the most important. Lynn, which stands at its mouth, handled most of England's trade with Normandy, Rhineland and Flanders until the beginning of the 18th century. In 1649 vessels carrying forty tons of freight could travel thirty-six miles up the Ouse from Lynn towards Cambridge at ordinary neap tides, and as far as Huntingdon with fifteen tons. Sturbridge Fair, at Cambridge, was for many years the greatest fair in

England. Foreign goods destined for Sturbridge were almost exclusively shipped first to Lynn, and then by barge along the Ouse to the River Cam which bordered the fairground.

The Witham. Prior to the Norman Conquest the Witham was a tideway navigation for ships to Lincoln. In 1121 Henry the First re-opened the Roman Foss Dyke to provide navigable communication between the Trent and the Witham so that the city of Lincoln might benefit from the improved trade.

The Yorkshire Ouse. Further north another important group of rivers flow into the Humber estuary. The Yorkshire Ouse, which joins the Trent to form the estuary, has been a major trade river for more than two thousand years. The city of York, which stands on its banks, was an international seaport until the 18th century. Vessels of any size could come within thirty miles of the city walls, and those up to eighty tons could reach the city itself.

The Trent. Up until the 18th century the Trent was a link in one of the most important communications routes between north and south Britain. Goods from the north were brought by pack-horse or waggon to Burton-on-Trent, barged down the Trent to Hull, and carried from there by sailing vessel to London. In medieval times the King's Messengers travelled along the Trent in preference to braving the dangers of Sherwood Forest. The Trent was, until the close of the 18th century, navigable by large vessels as high as Gainsborough.

The Idle. This river joins the Trent at Stockwith. Seven miles from its mouth lies the once famous port of Bawtry; today a sleepy little village, but once a major exporting centre.

The Thames. For more than two thousand years the Thames has been Britain's greatest trading river. Its tidal foreshores and riverbed between Teddington Lock and the sea hold many thousands of unrecovered relics. Roman finds can be made at Brentford, London Bridge and Wapping; medieval relics abound between Blackfriars and Southwark; while Victorian coins and jewellery await any mudlark who searches beneath any bridge from Kew to the Tower.

The Lea. This tributary of the Thames was described in 1424 as 'one of the greatest rivers of the Kingdom'. Its main port, Ware, has a long and colourful history.

The Medway. A very important river during the 18th century when Maidstone was a thriving port.

The Exe. Another river which has lost the battle with silt. In the 17th century cloth worth up to £100,000 was often sold in a single week at Exeter market which stood on its banks.

To most Londoners the banks of the Thames between Kew Bridge and Richmond Lock are pleasant spots for a Sunday stroll. To London's amateur treasure hunters they are a rich source of coins and relics from London's past. This treasure hunter is searching for relics in the water below the low tideline.

3 Buildings

Demolition sites

Thousands of Victorian houses are demolished every year in Britain to make way for new homes, office blocks and roadworks. They include a wide range of architectural styles from two-storey terraces, jerry-built around Victorian coalmines and factories, to detached, middle-class residences with mock-Grecian façades which have almost invariably ended their days carved into bed-sitters. The contractors who demolish them pause only to strip lead from roofs and plumbing systems and to make a hurried search for hidden money before each is razed to the ground with a few swings of a giant iron ball which destroys numerous antiques and pieces of collectable Victoriana every day simply because nobody takes the trouble to remove them before demolition begins. A brief survey of any 19th-century house reveals dozens of objects worth salvaging from destruction either because they are collected now or because they are likely to become collectors' items during the next few years as our Victorian town and city centres are transformed to cubes of concrete and glass.

Door furnishings, including knobs and knockers, have been collected for several years, yet only the largest brass examples likely to have worthwhile scrap value are removed by demolition men before a building is destroyed. When, as is often the case, the brass is hidden beneath several coats of dirty paint, the knob or knocker rarely merits a second glance from the contractor whose interests are confined to non-ferrous metals. Keyhole escutcheons, letterbox covers, boot scrapers and ornate door hinges are overlooked for the same reason.

Wrought-iron gates, railings and pipework are some of the fittings found outside the house which, on close inspection, often reveal superb Victorian craftsmanship. Little interest has so far been shown in them; nor in those ornate bricks, chimney

21

A south London demolition site. Just the place for a treasure hunt.

pots and coping stones seen on most 19th-century houses which must inevitably become rarities if the present rate of demolition continues. Inside the house there are wooden panels, decorative firebacks, iron stoves, kitchen tiles, taps and similar objects worth saving. The back garden is also likely to contain a Victorian household rubbish dump and one or two collectable garden ornaments.

Entire streets of houses such as this are now being demolished in every city and town. In order to search some of them for relics and bric-à-brac before they are pulled down you must first obtain permission from the demolition contractor working

22

in the street you have in mind. He is a busy man and will not take kindly to any interruption during working hours which prevents him getting on with the job. You are more likely to meet with a favourable reception if you visit the site around noon and wait until work stops for the lunch break which will probably be spent in a local pub. Talk to him then; offer to buy him a drink and ask if he can spare five minutes for a chat. Your chances of obtaining permission for a search will be greatly improved by this sort of approach. Explain your interest in Victoriana and impress upon the man that you are not intent on stripping lead from roofs or removing plumbing systems. If possible have with you one or two examples of the relics you hope to find—a doorknob, a boot scraper and an old bottle would be ideal. Show these to the contractor and tell him you will not interrupt his work if he allows you to search one or two of the houses further down the street which he and his men have not yet started to demolish.

I have always found that it pays to show the contractor the relics I have recovered at the end of each search. This serves to emphasize that objects removed are not those which usually interest him. If the haul is a good one I make a point of tipping the man a couple of pounds for his kindness, especially when there are other houses in the street which I hope to search at a later date. I recommend this policy to you.

Industrial sites

There has been in recent years a surge of interest in Britain's industrial past. Local history groups and preservation societies have saved and restored steam engines, looms, waterwheels and many other 19th-century machines which might otherwise have ended their days in scrapyards. Museums of industrial archaeology have been established in cities and towns once blackened and blighted by the Industrial Revolution as coal-mining, steel-making, ship-building, and other great industries of the Victorian era decline and disappear in our technological age. Matching this modern interest in old machines, which because of their size must usually be preserved in museums, is a sudden growth in the number of collectors who specialize in hand tools used by 19th-century tradesmen. Smiths' hammers, farm labourers' scythes, miners' lamps and helmets are all in demand as these trades and industries begin to fade into the pages of our history books.

Fortunately it is still possible to find examples of these old tools if one looks in the right places. In northern England, Scotland and Wales there are many hundreds of abandoned factory sites where they lie rusting in derelict workshops and forges. A polite letter to a local council or to the estate agent handling the sale of land occupied by such a site will rarely fail to bring permission for a search if you stress your interest in preserving and collecting old tools.

In moorland and mountainous regions where mining for metal ores once provided employment for thousands of people there is now an air of desolation. The veins of valuable ores were worked out long ago; now the machinery and buildings around the old shafts crumble with decay and heather is gradually covering the scars of industry. Search hereabouts and it will not take long to find an old miner's pick with a broken shaft which can soon be replaced, or a safety helmet which can be restored with a little paint and polish; or even a miner's lamp which a small repair will put back into working order. On most of these sites only the permission of the local farmer need be sought in order to carry out a search. Make sure you do not enter old mine shafts, which can be dangerous, and you will be able to spend a pleasant day in wild countryside while adding to your collection of industrial relics.

Farms

Farming today is a highly mechanized industry in which giant combines and tractors do most of the work formerly carried out by men and animals. This transition to complex machines has left in its wake a variety of hand tools, implements and horse

In moorland regions the sites of former lead mines are often indicated by decaying chimney stacks such as this.

24

trappings now gathering dust and rust on farms throughout Britain.

Most farmers will willingly allow you take away any you find in field corners or in barns and outhouses, but you must first obtain permission to carry out a search. There are few farmers who will refuse when you express interest in old farming methods. Some may turn out to be collectors themselves and may show you fine displays of sickles, scythes and other tools arranged on a farmhouse wall. If this turns out to be the case ask the farmer if he can direct you to a farm in the district where the tools are not collected. He is very likely to know of one.

4 Antique bottles

During the few years it has taken for bottle collecting to reach its present popularity as a hobby in Britain many thousands of bottles have been recovered from Victorian dumps. Their varieties of shape, colour, size, methods of manufacture and embossing have proved so numerous that research into their history and identification has not kept pace with the numbers coming out of the ground, even though most bottle collectors' clubs have spent a considerable amount of time on historical research.

A bottle 'swop meeting' organized by the London branch of the British Bottle Collectors' Club. Exchanging unwanted finds with other diggers is an excellent method of building up a collection.

26

The picture which emerges is, therefore, incomplete. It is not yet possible to date and identify accurately every bottle found. Nevertheless, much valuable information has been gathered by bottle-collecting enthusiasts from sources including old newspapers, directories and trade catalogues. This recorded information has provided a framework on which a history of Victorian bottles is now being put together; but it will take at least five more years of diligent digging and faithful recording of finds to complete the picture. You can help fill in those areas of the canvas which remain blank by joining a local club and by making sure that details of the bottles you find are added to the club's files. Meanwhile, the information available at the present time is summarized in this chapter.

Mineral waters

It is fortunate that the most interesting developments in mineral water bottle manufacture took place in the twenty years between 1870 and 1890. This coincides with the period during which unsorted household refuse was dumped in vast quantities in all parts of Britain and this have provided a plentiful supply of fascinating mineral water bottles for today's collectors.

The first artificial mineral waters were made by an Englishman named Joseph Priestley in 1772. Until the beginning of the 19th century they were sold in earthenware bottles with tight-fitting corks which had to be secured with wire or string to prevent gas pressure inside the bottles blowing them out. Corks often became dry and shrank after the bottles were filled, with the result that gases in the liquid escaped and the drink was spoiled.

It was not until 1809 that this problem was solved. In that year William Hamilton of Dublin patented a round-bottomed bottle which, after being filled with aerated liquid and corked, was stored on its side so that the cork remained permanently in contact with the liquid inside the bottle. The cork was thus kept moist and swollen and the risk of gas escape considerably reduced. Hamilton's original patent specification makes interesting reading:

'I generally use a glass or earthen bottle of a long ovate form, for several reasons, viz, not having a square bottom to stand upon, it can only lie on its side, of course, no leakage of air can take place, the liquid matter being always in contact with the stopper. . . .It can be much stronger than a bottle of equal weight made in the usual form, and is therefore better adapted for packaging, carriage, etc. . . I commonly stopper with cork, which, from the excessive pressure generally existing within the bottle, flies out on the detaining strings being cut.'

27

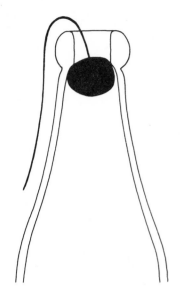

The first idea for an internally stoppered mineral water bottle: Johnson's india-rubber ball of 1864.

Left: The Barrett and Elers' patent of 1871; *right*: The stopper which Barrett and Elers eventually produced in large quantities.

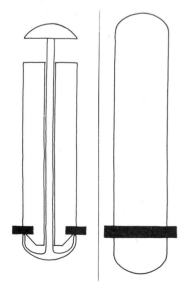

The Hamilton bottle achieved rapid and widespread popularity; it was used by most mineral water companies until the 1870s and by an ever-dwindling number until the early part of the 20th century. Its obvious disadvantage was that the round bottom, which solved the problem of dry corks, created a new problem for shopkeepers, publicans and customers because the bottle could not be placed on a flat surface. A less obvious problem was that the gassy liquid in the bottle was likely to spurt out of the neck when the wires or string holding the cork were cut.

It is interesting to note that although Hamilton writes in his specification of 'earthen' bottles very few have been recovered from Victorian dumps. The glass Hamilton was obviously far more popular. That the bottles were, as Hamilton claims, extremely strong is confirmed by the large numbers which survive intact in old dumps.

For more than fifty years the glass Hamilton with its wired-on cork reigned supreme as the container for aerated liquids; but as sales of bottled soda water, ginger beer and lemonade increased mineral water makers found the time-consuming job of securing corks far too costly. A new type of stopper was urgently needed.

In 1864 John Henry Johnson suggested the use of an india-rubber ball which was forced *inside* the bottle before the liquid was put into it. Gas pressure then held the ball against the inside of the neck and prevented the liquid spilling out. A piece of elastic wire was attached to the ball so that it could be pulled into position after the bottle was filled. The bottle was opened by pressing the ball slowly downwards so that gas could escape. When pressure inside the bottle was sufficiently reduced the india-rubber ball fell to the surface of the liquid where it floated as the contents were poured.

The Johnson stopper was the first in a long series of internal stoppers for mineral water bottles to be patented during the next twenty years. Those which came later were increasingly more complicated and *some* were more efficient; but all credit must go to John Henry Johnson who first thought of putting the stopper *inside* the bottle to obviate the need to secure it with wires or string. The inventions which followed were merely improvements on this very bright idea.

Johnson's india-rubber ball had two disadvantages: (a) if it became dry it allowed small amounts of gas to leak from the bottle; (b) because if floated in the liquid it often got in the way when the contents of the bottle were poured. The first of these disadvantages was tackled by retaining the round-bottomed Hamilton shape for the bottle, but this made it unpopular with publicans and shopkeepers.

In 1868 two inventors named Adams and Barrett patented a new type of internal stopper which consisted of a wooden plug with a trumpet-shaped end which had a groove into which an india-rubber washer could be fitted. The stopper was forced into the bottle which was then filled upside down. Because the stopper was made from wood having a greater specific gravity than water it sank through the liquid to the neck of the bottle where internal pressure from gas in the aerated water kept the washer firm against the neck. The bell-shaped end of the plug ensured a greater area of india-rubber pressing against the glass inside the neck than was possible with the Johnson ball. The stopper, which sank to the bottom of the bottle when gas pressure was released, did not therefore get in the way when the contents were poured.

Three years later, in 1871, Barrett and another inventor, C.G. Elers, improved on the Adams and Barrett stopper in a patent which described a wooded plug with an india-rubber washer at its lower end and a hole down its centre in which a wooden valve moved freely. When the bottle was filled with aerated liquid, gas pressure forced the valve against the india-rubber washer which in turn pressed against the inside of the bottle neck to create a gas-tight seal. To open the bottle the top of the sliding valve was first pressed down to relieve gas pressure. The wooden plug then fell to the bottom of the bottle and the contents were poured.

No examples of this type of stopper have so far been recovered from dumps. It seems unlikely that it was ever widely used, though Barrett and Elers did manufacture a simplified version without the inner valve which was extremely popular.

Its greatest rival was patented on 3 September 1872. On that day Hiram Codd of Camberwell perfected his globe-stoppered mineral water bottle which was soon to achieve world-wide acclaim. The final shape of the bottle and its unique closure took Codd more than a year to develop. As early as November 1870 he patented the invention of a bottle which had an annular groove formed inside the neck during manufacture. A glass marble was placed inside the bottle before the neck was finished and, when the glass had cooled, an india-rubber washer was fitted into the annular groove. When the bottle was filled with aerated water the glass marble was forced by gas pressure against the washer in the annular groove to form a gas-tight seal. If we compare this method of closure with Johnson's india-rubber ball of 1864 we see that it was Codd's idea of an annular groove which provided the breakthrough in closure developments—*not* the ball stopper.

Nine months later, in August, 1871, Codd developed his invention further by patenting a similar bottle with a recess in its neck to hold the glass marble while the contents of the bottle were poured. In the same specification he claimed patent rights on a stopper which was an improvement on the Barrett and Elers wooden plug. One disadvantage of their plug was that

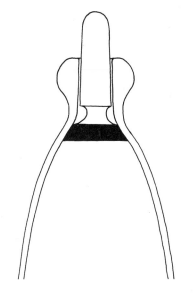

The Adams and Barrett stopper of 1868.

Drawings from Hiram Codd's specification of 1872.

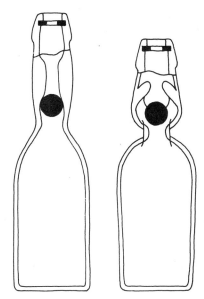

it had to be longer than the internal diameter of the bottle to prevent it turning upside down when it was pushed into the bottle. Codd claimed that by having a recess in the neck of his bottle he was able to use a much shorter plug and thus make a considerable saving in the cost of wood for stoppers—an indication of the fierce competition between mineral water bottle makers in those days!

In the final specification on 3 September 1872 Codd perfected his bottle by adding projecting ridges inside the neck of the bottle to guide the glass marble to the side of the neck so that it did not interfere with pouring.

The scene was now set for a mammoth struggle between dozens of inventors who patented hundreds of internal stoppers for mineral water bottles during the next few years. Many of the ideas put forward merely suggested slight modifications to the wooden plug and the glass marble, some specified different materials, others were quite impractical and never got further than the drawing board. Those which went into production included the following:

Aylesbury's stopper of 1875 consisted of two india-rubber washers on a metal spindle. The lower washer was firmly attached to the spindle and formed a gas-tight seal in the usual way at the bottom of the neck. The upper washer was loose on the spindle and was made to fit tightly into the lip of the bottle. To open the bottle the spindle was pressed downwards to move the lower washer. Escaping gas then blew out the upper washer to allow the contents to be poured.

Vallet's stopper of the same year consisted of a short wooden stem, cone-shaped at its lower end. An india-rubber washer rested on the cone and was forced by gas pressure against the lower part of the bottle neck. A second washer was held in a groove at the other end of the stem; this provided an additional gas seal in the upper part of the bottle neck.

Sutcliffe and Fewing's bobbin-shaped stopper of 1876 was made from glass and sheathed by a tube of india-rubber. The mouth of the bottle into which this stopper fitted was moulded with a deep internal projection against which the india-rubber covering of the stopper rested to form a gas-tight seal. The bottle was also moulded with an internal projection around the lower shoulders which held the stopper while the contents were poured.

Lamont, Rose, Sykes, Tapp, Breffit, Edwards, Cherry, Edmonds, Nuttall, Macvay, Trotman, Deeks and many others also invented stoppers which were produced commercially; but two names—Codd and Rylands—stand out as the most important in the fascinating history of internal stoppers. Together they account for more than half of the millions of mineral water bottles produced during the last thirty years of the 19th century.

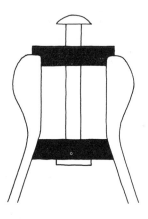

Aylesbury's stopper of 1875.

Vallet's stopper of 1875.

Hiram Codd's globe-stoppered bottle with its ingenious annular groove and neck crimpings achieved rapid popularity when introduced to the mineral water trade in 1872. Within a year Codd had issued manufacturing licences to more than fifty glass-makers throughout Britain, and by the end of 1873 these companies and Codd's own works at Camberwell were producing tens of thousands of globe-stoppered bottles. To stimulate even wider use Codd soon began issuing free manufacturing licences to glass-makers on condition that they purchased supplies of glass marbles and india-rubber rings from Codd's own company.

One of these early licensed manufacturers was Ben Rylands of Barnsley who founded the Hope Glass Works there in 1867. He adopted as his trade mark the figure '4' which was embossed on bottles produced by his company to signify the four qualities which Ben Rylands believed to be of utmost importance in bottle manufacture—neatness, cleanliness, accuracy and strength. Certainly accuracy in moulding and strength of glass were essential in the manufacture of Codd's bottles, and those made by Ben Rylands were soon in great demand. By 1876 the entire Hope Glass Works was devoted to their manufacture and in the following year Hiram Codd ceased manufacture at Camberwell and became a partner in Ryland's Barnsley company.

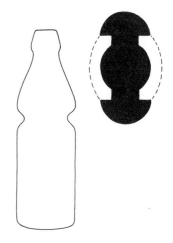

Sutcliffe and Fewing's invention of 1876.

Three globe-stoppered mineral water bottles made by Dan Rylands of Barnsley—the Premier, the Bulb and the Valve.

31

Mid-Victorian mineral water bottles. The marble-stoppered bottle on the left has lugs on both sides of its neck. It was made by William Barnard of London before 1900, probably under licence from Dan Rylands. The other two bottles shown are examples of Nuttall's patent of 1878.

An early sealed wine bottle.

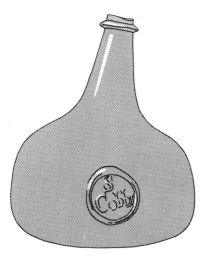

The two men worked well together. Codd's inventive genius and Ryland's skills as a glass-maker and businessman assured the company's success. Within a year globe-stoppered bottles made by Rylands and Codd were in use throughout the world. Millions were exported to the United States, Canada, South Africa, India, Australia, New Zealand and every other country in which mineral waters were popular. In the face of this overwhelming competition most of the company's rivals either went out of business or sought manufacturing licences for Codd's bottles.

Three years later, in 1881, Ben Rylands died suddenly and his son, Dan, became an equal partner with Hiram Codd in ownership of the company. Like his father, Dan Rylands was a skilled glass-maker and an astute businessman. He was also a brilliant inventor, determined to put into practice some of his own ideas for improving the bottles which had made the company world famous. Codd bitterly resented this interference in matters which he regarded as his sole prerogative; it was not long before personal rivalry between the two began to affect the efficient running of the company. Their stormy co-partnership lasted until 1884 when Codd sold out his share of the business and his patent rights to the younger man and returned to Camberwell.

With Codd out of the way Dan Rylands set about improving the globe-stoppered bottles made at Barnsley and quickly revealed a genius for invention at least equal to that of his former partner. He improved on the original Codd by patenting a bottle which could be inclined both ways for pouring; he introduced another which had two additional indents in the neck to keep the stopper in a fixed position when the bottle was cleaned; and he patented a third which had a small glass valve in its shoulder which was pressed to release gas pressure. Under his guidance the company prospered until the 1890s when the great era of internally stoppered bottles began to draw to a close. Before the end of the century many mineral water companies had progressed to bottles with screw stoppers, though globe-stoppered variations on Hiram Codd's original idea were used in country districts until the 1920s.

Wines, beers and spirits

Bottles with glass seals on their shoulders into which owner's names or initials were impressed were commonly used for wines and beers throughout the 18th century, but they had gone out of fashion before the period of large-scale refuse dumping in late Victorian times. Those few which are found in the late 19th-century dumps are usually of foreign manufacture; you are more likely to find examples of early sealed bottles by hunting in the mud of rivers which flow through large towns and cities. The majority of wine bottles found by dump diggers are dark

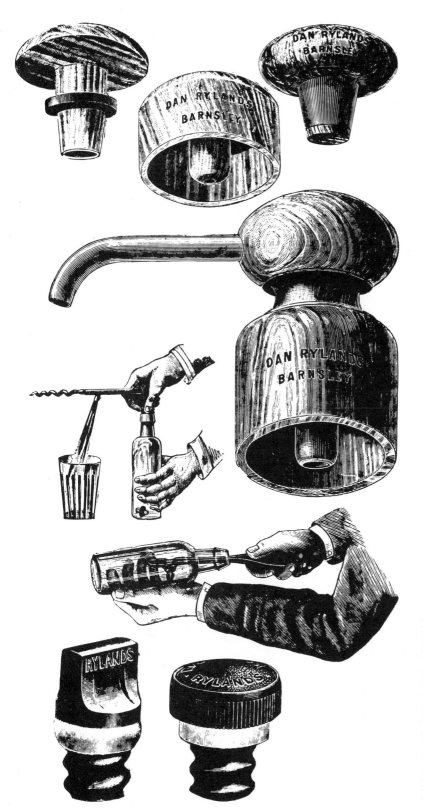

Top: Openers for globe-stoppered bottles. Some mineral water makers gave them away; others supplied them to shopkeepers who kept one chained to the counter. *Centre*: Combined openers and syphons which allowed the bottle to be opened and poured without fear of splashing. The model on the left was also fitted with a corkscrew. Below is a tool used to extract internal stoppers from bottles. *Bottom*: Screw stoppers which eventually replaced internal stoppers.

Bottles like these are *not* found in the 20th-century rubbish dumps. They are *possible* finds on sites where dumping took place before 1880. *Left*: A sealed wine bottle; *centre*: An earthenware stout bottle; *right*: A sealed beer bottle.

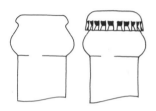

Above: The crown stopper was invented by an American William Painter in 1892. It was not widely used in Britain before 1903. *Below*: A beer bottle with seal. The shape is typical of beer bottles made before 1850.

green and unembossed—not unlike their modern counterparts.

19th-century beers are, on the other hand, almost always richly embossed with ornate trade marks and brewery names. The glass is usually dark brown or dark green and closures used include corks, swing stoppers with wire fasteners and internal screws. The crown cap, which is found on most modern beer bottles, came into use in 1903.

Gin was a popular drink in Victorian England. It was usually sold in square bottles of dark green or brown glass which were often embossed with the name of a Dutch gin distiller. Whisky and other spirits came in coffin-shaped flasks or in round, flat bottles known as pumpkin seeds. In Scotland and Ireland glass whisky bottles were uncommon, stoneware flasks being widely used.

Many public houses also sold spirits in round and oblong flasks on which the name of the pub and occasionally the name of the publican were embossed or etched with acid on the surface of the glass. Railway companies, large hotels and other organizations which sold alcoholic drinks also used this form of advertising on their bottles. Historical events such as coronations and famous people including politicians and folk heroes were often depicted on embossed whisky flasks. While digging a Victorian dump in Sunderland, County Durham recently I found an oblong flask embossed with a picture of a man nailing a flag to the mast of a ship. This was Jack Crawford, hero of the Battle of Camperdown which was fought in 1798 by the British and Dutch navies. Jack Crawford climbed the mast of his ship to re-hoist the British flag after Dutch cannon fire sent it

34

Left: Victorian whisky bottles. The coffin flask on the right records in its embossing that Mr Sambrook was once landlord of the 'Brick-layers' Arms', Old Kent Road. *Above*: Embossed whisky flask. *Below*: Folk heroes and famous battles were common subjects as trade marks on whisky bottles.

crashing to the deck. This action earned Jack a medal and a hero's welcome when he returned to his home town of Sunderland.

Poisons

There were few controls on the sale of toxic substances to the general public in the 19th century. Arsenic, belladonna, strychnine and other deadly poisons were all sold to anyone who required them and this inevitably resulted in hundreds of fatal cases of accidental poisoning every year.

Inventions to reduce the risk of poisonous liquids being drunk included such ideas as a bottle with a stopper which could be locked and a poison bottle storage cabinet from which bottles could only be removed with the aid of a special key. These and other mechanical inventions were widely used in hospitals but they were too costly to be put into general use. Other ideas which were put into use included a three-sided bottle and a bottle on which a skull and crossbones were embossed; but the two methods of identification which achieved widespread popularity were the moulding of vertical lines and sharp projections on the bottle's outer surfaces. Such bottles could be readily identified by sight and touch, both essential precautions at a time when many people were illiterate and when lighting in houses was so primitive that most people would have preferred to grope in darkness for their medicines if they required them at night rather than go to the trouble of lighting an oil lamp or a gas mantle. As a further aid to identification cobalt blue glass was used for more dangerous

JACK CRAWFORD 1797 HERO 1797 CAMPERDOWN

"SHOULDER TO SHOULDER"
ST GEORGE'S KEY BATTLE
1798   1898
COMMEMORATION
FINE OLD SCOTCH WHISKY
BOTTLED BY D. FINDLATER & C°. GLASGOW

The Martin Poison Bottle was designed to fit into a special storage rack with a bar which fitted the recess in the bottle's shoulder. The bar could be locked to prevent removal of the bottle. The triangular bottle (*right*) was used to identify poisonous liquids.

From the shelves of a Victorian chemist's shop: Warner's Safe Cure; Old Doctor Townsend's Sarsaparilla Blood Purifier; Lorne Pomade and Hair Curler; Daffy's Elixir.

substances and dark green glass for mild poisons. The words NOT TO BE TAKEN were also embossed on the side of the bottle.

Medicine bottles

There was no National Health Service in Victorian Britain; only the very rich could afford the services of surgeons and doctors whose fees were beyond the reach of most of the population. Poorer folk relied heavily on the local chemist's shop where potions and pills which claimed to cure every ailment from cholera to a bald head could be bought. Most of the bottles which contained these medicines were embossed with amusing trade marks or advertising claims and they are much sought after by today's bottle collectors.

Victorian quacks and confidence tricksters made handsome profits selling worthless concoctions to a gullible public only too ready to believe in anything which might temporarily alleviate their aches and pains. Some sold 'cure-alls' which claimed to work miracles on any ailment in the medical dictionary; others sold 'specifics' which limited their healing properties to one particular condition.

William Radams sold a 'cure-all' under the trade name of 'Microbe Killer' which, according to the embossing on the beautiful brown bottle in which it was sold, destroyed germs, bacteria and fungus. One side of the bottle was embossed with a picture of a man with a large club attacking a skeleton; beneath the picture were the words, 'Cures all diseases'. When public

36

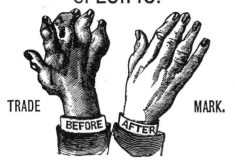

ALARCON DE MARBELLA'S
SPECIFIC.

TRADE   BEFORE AFTER   MARK.

SAFE

SAFE

health authorities analyzed Radam's liquid in 1903 it was found to consist of 99.3% water, 0.1% sulphuric acid and 0.6% coal ash!

Another famous quack was Doctor H.H. Warner who sold his medicine in dark green and dark brown bottles embossed with a picture of a large iron safe. He called his product 'Safe Cure' and his advertising claimed the liquid was a certain remedy for Bright's disease, urinary disorders, female complaints, general debility, malaria and all diseases caused by disordered kidneys and livers. Later analysis revealed that it was, in fact, little more than coloured water.

Trade marks embossed on medicine bottles. *Top row:* Gout Cure (T. Mills & Son), Cure-all (H.H.Warner), Salve (Benjamin Booth). *Bottom row:* Toothache Cure (Teasdale & Co), Cure-all (W. Radams).

Babies' feeding bottles

Contrary to popular belief, not all our great-grandparents were breast-fed babies. The large numbers of feeding bottles which have been unearthed in Victorian dumps confirm that they were widely used during the latter part of the 19th century. The commonest shape found is a flattened and slightly elongated dome with a short neck. Later examples are more elongated and look rather like Hamilton bottles with flat bases. Upright examples are occasionally found, but the double-ended 'banana'

SPLITTING FOR A HEAD-ACHE!

DISEASE FLEEING FROM CARBOLINE

HAMLIN'S WIZARD OIL

For Internal and External Use

CURES

Rheumatism,
Lame Back,
Headache,
Neuralgia,
Toothache,
Earache,
Sore Throat,
Diphtheria,
Catarrh,
Inflammation of
the Kidneys, and
All Painful Affections.

None genuine without this
fac-simile of signature on wrapper

ELECTRIC
HAIR PRODUCER AND RESTORER

shape common today does not seem to have been popular before the beginning of this century.

All Victorian feeders were designed to stand on a flat surface during use. Nursing one's baby during feeding was not the common practice. Instead a glass tube was fitted inside the bottle and passed through the stopper whch was made from cork, wood, porcelain, tin, or glass. A rubber pipe with a teat at one end was fitted over the glass tube and the bottle was then placed in a position where the teat end of the pipe could reach the baby's mouth. Some models were made with air vents to prevent collapse of the tube as the baby sucked its milk.

(*Opposite*) *Left to right:* Hop Bitters Company's Headache Cure, Henry Ellison's Carboline Germ Destroyer, Hamlin Brothers' Rubbing Oil, Standard Drug Company's Electric Hair Restorer.

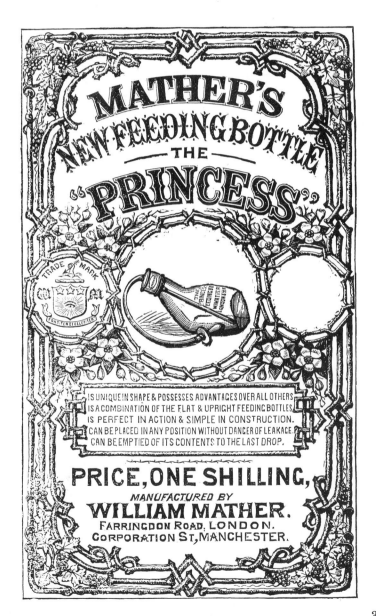

This 1887 advertisement for a feeding bottle shows the tube to which the teat was attached.

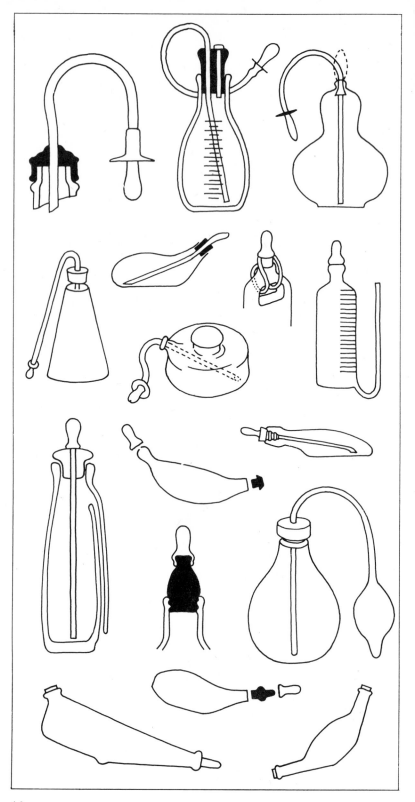

A variety of feeding bottle shapes
patented between 1870 and 1910.

Fascinating finds made by a member of the British Bottle Collectors' Club during a group-dig on a Victorian refuse site on the outskirts of London.

Four highly-prized Victorian bottles. Left to right: Daffy's Elixir; Price's Patent Candle Co's Glycerine; Radams' Microbe Killer; a cobalt-blue castor oil bottle.

Beautiful rubbish! These multi-coloured pot lids were thrown into Victorian dustbins when the contents of the fish- and meat-paste pots they covered had been eaten.

Fire grenades

The forerunner of the modern fire extinguisher was a small glass bottle filled with carbon tetrachloride which was thrown into the centre of a fire where it broke to allow its contents to put out the flames. These fire grenades were placed in metal racks on the walls of hotels, offices and public buildings to be ready for instant use if the building caught fire. They were popular throughout the late Victorian period and did not disappear entirely until the 1920s when metal fire extinguishers came into general use. The bottles were usually round, 4 in. to 6 in. in diameter, and the glass was blue, green or amber. Less common were the 'stick grenade' types which were cylindrical and 12 in. to 15 in. long.

Syphons

Syphons for aerated waters were popular during the late Victorian period when two varieties were in general use: the double-globe seltzogene which was used for making seltzer water and the cylindrical syphon used to dispense soda water and other aerated drinks.

Seltzogenes were purchased by customers who wished to make their own mineral waters. They were usually covered with fine wire mesh to protect the glass from damage. Seltzer salts, tartaric acid and bicarbonate of soda were placed inside the bottle, and the glass tube and metal tap screwed into position.

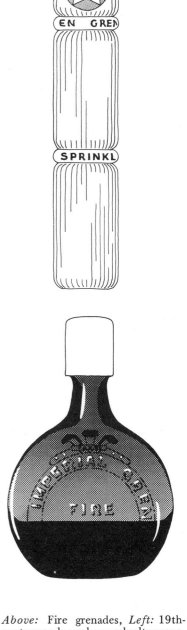

Above: Fire grenades, *Left:* 19th-century soda syphon and seltzogene.

41

Water was then injected into the bottle through a valve at the rear of the tap to produce the drink inside the bottle. The liquid was drawn off by depressing a lever on the tap.

Cylindrical syphons were sold ready-filled with soda water and other effervescent drinks. The customer returned his syphon to the mineral water works for re-charging when empty. These bottles differ only slightly in shape from modern syphons but Victorian examples were usually made from coloured glass and the taps are of pewter or tin. Modern syphons are made from clear glass and they have plastic or stainless steel taps.

'Figurals'

A figural is a bottle moulded in the shape of an animal, bird, human figure or an inanimate object. Today their use is confined almost exclusively to cosmetics, but during the 19th century and until at least the 1930s they were occasionally used for whisky, wine and other alcoholic drinks. Several varieties have been found including violins, mermaids and knights on horseback, but little is known about the companies who used them. They seem likely to have been used on special occasions; perhaps to mark a whisky distiller's centenary year, or to bottle wine of an exceptional vintage.

Figural bottles.

Inks

In the days of the quill, long before ball-point pens and cartridge refills, vast quantities of ink were sold by stationers and chemists. Ink bottles found their way into every household dustbin and all Victorian dumps contain large numbers of these interesting containers. In 1880 a bottle of ink cost two or three pence; ink bottles were, therefore, made as cheaply as possible from crude glass and in simple two-piece moulds. To keep costs to a minimum the glass-maker formed the mouth of the bottle by simply cutting it from the blowpipe end of the mould to leave a jagged or sheared lip. Its sharp edges bit into the cork to form an efficient closure.

Food bottles and jars

During the latter part of the 19th century a wide range of glass bottles and jars were used to package foods sold in grocery stores. The majority of these containers were unembossed and the glass used to make them was of a pale shade of green. Clearer glass was used after 1900 when food manufacturers began to use containers which allowed the housewife to see the product inside the bottle or jar. The wide variety of bottle shapes used for these products is indicated by the accompanying page from the catalogue of a late Victorian glassworks.

Decorative sauce bottles found in an 1890s dump.

43

FRENCH JAM JAR.

4-lb. JAM JAR
WITH PATENT CAP.

HALF-GALLON PICKLE
JAR.

2-lb. JAM JAR.

JAM OR PICKLE
JAR.

PICKLE OR
SAUCE.

PATENT
WHOLE FRUIT JAR.

OLIVE QUART.

2-lb. JAM JAR.

PRESERVED PEA
JAR.

HEXAGON WALNUT.

PRESERVED MEAT
JAR.

SQUARE PICKLE.

Pickles were extremely popular one hundred years ago. These jars held pickled onions and picalilli.

Earthenware

Bottles made from brown, salt-glazed stoneware were used in England for wines and ales as early as the 16th century. Until 1684 they were all imported from Germany but in that year kilns were established at Fulham, and shortly afterwards, when other potteries commenced at Nottingham, Lambeth and Derby, this continental trade ceased altogether. From then until the 1860s English potteries were in keen competition with glass-makers as suppliers of containers for a wide range of liquids and foods.

The majority of these earthenware bottles and jars were made at the group of potteries at Lambeth, the important makers being James Stiff, Stephen Green & Co. and Doultons (who traded at Doulton & Watts until 1858). Joseph Bourne of the Denby Pottery near Derby was the largest manufacturer in the provinces. The containers these firms produced included whisky flasks, gin bottles, blacking pots, ink bottles, meat and fish paste jars, hot water bottles and many others; but towards the end of the 19th century much of this trade was lost to glass-makers. By the time of the great refuse disposal period during the 1880s the potters' share of the market had dwindled to blacking, vinegar, ink and ginger beer bottles. Of these the blacking and ink bottles are uninteresting, being dull brown in colour and bearing only incised pottery marks; but the varieties of shape and colour in the ginger beer bottles more than makes up for this shortcoming.

45

A fine collection of ginger beers.

The most sought-after ginger beers are those with underglaze transfers. These came into general use after 1880 when potteries were obliged to compete with glass-makers who were at that time making their glass bottles more attractive with rich embossing and, later, with colourful paper labels. The potters' answer to this competition was ginger beer bottles in pleasing colours with striking transfers depicting ginger beer makers' trade marks. Many of the bottles were given two colours: the body might be white or yellow to contrast with the black transfer while the shoulders and neck were coloured dark brown, green or blue.

Until the end of the 19th century most ginger beers had cork stoppers which were firmly secured with wires or string. After 1900 an increasing number of ginger beer makers began to favour bottles with internal screw stoppers. These were used in country districts until at least the 1920s when public taste for ginger beer began to wane as more fruit-flavoured fizzy drinks, which were sold in glass bottles to allow the customer to see the appetizing colours, came onto the market.

Dating bottles

Very few Victorian bottle-makers marked their products with the year of manufacture, though many used numerical and alphabetical codes by which they alone could tell the month and year in which a bottle was made. The code was usually embossed on the base of the bottle and, if it happens to be a numerical code, it can mislead beginners at bottle collecting who sometimes interpret the figures as a date. Recently a newcomer to the hobby showed me a Codd-type, globe-stoppered bottle which had the figures '1843' embossed on its base. He was quite disappointed when I explained that this was a code which told the original bottle-maker the date of manufacture, but that the bottle could not have been made in 1843 because such bottles were not invented until 1872. A closer inspection revealed further embossing which read, 'Sole maker. D. Rylands, Barnsley.' This proved that the bottle could not have been made before 1884, the year in which Dan Rylands became sole proprietor of the Barnsley company. The bottle was a Codd 'Original' and Dan Rylands' catalogue for 1891 states that this particular type of globe-stoppered bottle 'is not now recommended'. I was, therefore, able to tell the owner of the bottle that it was probably manufactured between 1884 and 1891.

Two stone ginger beer bottles. The one on the left was made before 1900 and the one on the right is dated 1913.

There are other clues to a bottle's date of manufacture which can be found by examining the bottle closely. If the faint lines or seams on its surface which indicate the positions of mould joints extend from the base to the very top of the bottle's lip it must obviously have been made in a mould which produced a complete bottle in one moulding operation. Such manufacturing techniques were not used before the beginning of the 20th century; any bottle which has seams along its entire length is unlikely to be of Victorian origin.

Prior to 1900 it was common practice to mould the body, shoulders and neck of the bottle in one operation and then to apply the lip around the neck of the bottle after it had been removed from the mould. In the absence of further dating evidence it is reasonable to assume that such 'applied lip' bottles were made in the 19th century. Mould seams will always stop short of the lip on such bottles.

During the 1880s there was a vogue for bottles made in three-piece moulds which enabled the body of the bottle to be blown without producing unsightly mould marks. The mould which formed the body was a metal or wooden cylinder closed at one end. The body was blown inside this cylinder and withdrawn from the open end. Two further moulds which formed the shoulders and neck were then positioned at the top

47

Much useful information about bottles and their uses can be gleaned by studying contemporary advertisements: *Below:* medicine bottle (Coqueluche Co) fire grenade (Spong & Co); *opposite:* glue pot (Field and Tuer), bitters bottle (Hortwig Kantorowicz), sauce bottle (Courtenay & Co), round champagne bottle (Green & Co), smelling salts bottle (F.R. Roe), tonic water bottle (J.G. Webb).

of the body and more glass was used to produce the top part of the bottle. Thus the bottle was made in three pieces—one body and two halves of shoulder and neck—and the vertical seams on its surface extend from beneath the applied lip to its shoulders. Such 'three-piece mould' bottles can be dated to the 1880s if there is no other evidence to suggest a different date.

Hand-made, 17th-century bottles were free-blown without the use of moulds. The glass blower simply blew a sphere of glass to the correct size to form the body of the bottle. During the 18th century when bottles with vertical sides came into general use the glass blower used an open-ended cylinder of wood to shape the parellel sides of the bottle. He turned the bottle on his blowing rod as it was shaped; this gave the body vertical sides but it did not produce mould seams.

In order to form a neat lip on such free-blown bottles it was necessary to remove the partly formed bottle from the blowing rod and to smooth the jagged mouth thus created. A second glass blower, usually an apprentice, would take a solid iron rod, known as a 'pontil', and attach it to the bottom of the bottle. The first glass blower could then break off his blowing rod and smooth the lip while the apprentice turned the red-hot bottle on his pontil. Because the pontil left a rough scar on the bottom of the bottle it became common practice to produce a concave base by pushing the pontil rod inwards while the glass was still soft. This 'kick-up' is still produced today on wine bottles even though it is unnecessary to do so, because wine bottles are now made in two-piece moulds on machines which can turn out hundreds of bottles in the time it took to make a single free-blown specimen.

An interesting method of dating embossed Victorian bottles is to look for contemporary advertisements in Victorian newspapers and magazines which either illustrate the bottle you have found or tell you what it originally contained. Most towns have at least one newspaper which commenced publication before 1900. Its file of back copies will be a storehouse of information on bottles you recover from local Victorian rubbish dumps.

The Trade Marks Registration Act of 1875 made it compulsory for any company which claimed exclusive use of a particular trade mark to record its mark at the Trade Marks Registry Office in Chancery Lane, London. Each application for registration was recorded in a weekly journal which was on sale to the public so that any person who wished to object to a particular mark being used by a company could do so before the mark was officially registered. The application had to show a drawing of the trade mark, the name and address of the applicant, the date of the application and the length of time the mark had been used prior to that date. This law relating to the registration of trade marks is in force today and the weekly

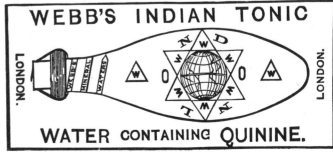

THE SPARKLING SPRING.

SODA WATER

ROYAL TUNBRIDGE WELLS SPA.
TRADE   MARK.
MINERAL   SPRING
PURITY
R. TUDDENHAM.

C   M
&   Co.
P   &   G.

SLIP

COCKCROFT'S
TRADE MARK.
MINERAL WATERS

FRUIT
ALES

TRADE MARK

THE OXFORD
MINERAL WATERS COMPY

journal is still issued. So far more than nine million trade marks have been registered; the first to be entered on the list was the Bass Triangle known to all beer drinkers.

More than two hundred thousand trade marks were registered in the 19th century and many bottle collectors' clubs have purchased complete sets of the weekly *Trade Marks Journal* covering the period 1875-1903 for their libraries. By using these records in conjunction with local trades directories and newspaper advertisements it is possible to date many Victorian bottles within a year or so of their manufacture.

The British Bottle Collectors' Club has formulated a research procedure for dating any bottle not already recorded on club files. It is not an infallible procedure, but I recommend it to you as a method of research which, in addition to helping you date some of your finds, will teach you much about Victorian bottles and the products they contained.

Bottle collectors' research procedure

1. Before attempting to date the bottles you find on a dump make every effort to establish the period during which the site was used for refuse disposal. If you can obtain this information, and if the period of dumping covers only two or three years, you will know the approximate age of every object you find in the dump. Likely sources of such information are council records and elderly local residents.

2. If the above information is unobtainable confirm that the majority of glass bottles in the dump have applied lips and mould seams which stop short of the top of the bottle. If they have both your dump was almost certainly in use during the 19th century.

3. When examining a single glass bottle look for an applied lip, air bubbles and greenish glass. If the bottle has all three it is probably Victorian. If it has an external screw top, mould seams which extend to the lip and it is made from clear, bubble-free glass it is almost certainly not Victorian.

4. If you find a bottle which has no mould seams made from glass of any shade of green and which has a 'kick-up' in its base it *could* be an early free-blown wine bottle dating from before 1850; but this is most unlikely. Late 19th-century wine bottles of French, Spanish and Portuguese origin were made without mould seams by turning the bottle in the mould as it was blown to give the finished bottle an attractive shine. Such foreign mould-blown wines have a symmetry not found in free-blown bottles and they do not have a rough pontil scar at the top of the 'kick-up'.

Most Victorian mineral water makers had elaborate trade marks which they embossed on their bottles.
Above: James Swanzy, Liverpool (1876). *Opposite:* Benjamin Wells, Forest Hill, Kent (1878), George Gulliver, Aylesbury, Bucks (1877), Richard Tuddenham, Tunbridge Wells, Kent (1871), Charles Mumby, Gosport, Hants (1876), Edward Handslip, South Shields, Co. Durham (1886), Savage & Son, Mansfield, Notts (1881), Thomas Cockcroft, Birkenhead, Ches. (1856), Bird & Co, High Holborn, Middx (1880), Wilmer & Sons, Newport Pagnell, Bucks (1859), Julius Peters, Hull, Yorks (1876), Richard Evans, Wrexham, Denbighs (1873), Oxford Mineral Water Co, Oxford (1876). (*Dates in brackets show year in which trade mark was first used.)

Pencil rubbings like these are made by members of the British Bottle Collectors' Club so that details about bottles recovered from old dumps can be recorded.

5. If the bottle has a glass seal on its shoulder examine it carefully to confirm that it is a true seal which has been impressed into a blob of glass added to the bottle after it was blown. Some late 19th-century bottle-makers imitated seals by moulding them on their bottles. If it is a true seal you have a choice find.

6. If you find a bottle with embossed lettering or a trade mark check local newspapers for advertising issued by the company. Be on the look-out for changes in the company's name. If you find a bottle embossed 'William Smith & Son' try to establish by studying contemporary advertising whether or not the company ever traded as 'William Smith' and when the son became a partner in the business.

7. If your local club has copies of the *Trade Marks Journal* and your bottle is embossed with a registered trade mark you will be able to find out the date on which the mark was first used and the address at which the company traded when the mark was registered. This last information can be checked against local 19th-century street and trades directories which are usually available at public libraries. By checking these directories at three or five-yearly intervals it is often possible to establish the year in which the company went out of business.

8. Similar research can be carried out on earthenware bottles and jars which have pottery marks and transfer-printed or incised registered trade marks.

9. You should always make detailed notes on any bottles you identify. Record company name changes, sizes of bottles used by a company, what the products were that the bottles contained, selling prices and any other useful information. Make two copies of these notes and pass one copy to the secretary of your local club.

Bottle prices
Inability to dig one's own bottles out of the ground because of lack of time or other considerations does not rule out the possibility of owning a beautiful collection. There are numerous bottle shops and antique stalls throughout the country where any reader may buy excellent specimens—often the very best of those found by diggers who spend their time keeping the retail outlets supplied with fresh stocks. It is possible to acquire a collection of more common bottles for a few pounds, though higher prices must, of course, be paid for rarities.

The following price guide, based on a survey of dealers' lists during the past year, is divided into four sections to indicate rarity and relative values. Section one contains a selection of the most common bottles which can be bought for less than £1.00 each. Section two includes some of the popular bottles on sale at less than £3.00 each; while Section Three lists some of those which all bottle buffs are eager to add to their collections and which sell at £3.00 to £10.00. They are difficult to find; they are very likely to increase in value. Section Four contains some of the bottles which are recognized throughout the bottle-collecting world as highly prized specimens—extremely rare, exceptionally beautiful, most reluctantly disposed of by those fortunate enough to dig them out of the ground. Prices in this section usually range from £10.00 to £30.00.

Bottles in section one are unlikely to increase in value during the next few years no matter how popular bottle collecting becomes. There are far too many in the ground for them to become rarities until all accessible dumps are exhausted. Those listed in the other three sections *must* rise in price as demand begins to overtake supply; but differentials will be maintained. If a bottle in Section Three which now sells at £5.00 rises in price to £10.00 during the next year, then prices in sections two and four will also double.

Section one: bottles at less than £1.00

Inks — eight-sided, aqua, unembossed; boat, aqua, unembossed; earthenware, all sizes
Poisons — four-sided, blue or green, embossed NOT TO BE TAKEN
Mineral waters — screw-stoppered, green, embossed with trade marks; Hamilton flat-bottomed, aqua
Beers — screw-stoppered, green or brown, embossed with trade marks
Sauces — four-sided, aqua
Pickle jars — four-sided, aqua
Ginger beers — earthenware, incised marks
Blacking pots — earthenware, all sizes
Earthenware jars — white glaze, all sizes
Oxo/Bovril — light brown
Valentine's meat juice — brown

Section two: bottles at £1.00—£3.00

Inks — blue or dark green
Poisons — three-sided, blue or green; round, small, blue or green
Mineral waters — globe-stoppered, aqua; Hamilton round-bottomed, aqua; embossed FARTHING DEPOSIT ON THIS BOTTLE
Ginger beers — earthenware, underglaze transfers
Beers — spring-stoppered, green or brown, embossed
Spa waters — Apollinaris, earthenware, all sizes
Wines — EMU brand

Hair restorers
Hot water bottles — earthenware
Medicines — white glass
Pickle jars — eight-sided, embossed

Section three: bottles at £3.00–£10.00

Inks — bell-shaped, blue; boat-shaped, blue or dark green
Poisons — round, large, blue or green
Sauces — fluted, aqua
Beers — black, embossed
Bottles bearing a Registered Design mark
Mineral waters — internal stoppers, patented designs
Earthenware jars — white, underglaze transfers
Cod liver oils — blue, embossed
'Quack' cures — blue or brown, embossed DOCTOR, CURE or
    SPECIFIC
Mexican Hair Renewer — blue
Bailey's Goutine — aqua
Spirits flasks — pumpkin seed; coffin
19th-century bottles bearing original labels

Section four: bottles priced above £10.00

Warner's 'Safe' Cure
Warner's 'Log cabin' bitters
Zara Maraschino Liqueur
Inks — cottage
Daffy's Elixir
Price's Patent Candle Company — blue
Radam's Microbe Killer — brown
Dr Townsend's Sarsaparilla
Wines and beers bearing shoulder or neck seals
Caster oils — blue
Mineral waters — globe-stoppered, made by Hiram Codd of
    Camberwell before 1877; globe-stoppered, made by Ben
    Rylands; internal stoppers, Barrett and Elers' patent; internal
    stoppers, blue, brown, dark green
Whiskies — earthenware, underglaze transfers
Figurals — applied lips
Syphons — blue, dark green, amber
Codd-Hamilton hybrids
Feeding bottles — pre-1910
Sauces — fluted, blue

5 Discovering pot lids

Prior to the second half of the 18th century decoration was applied to pottery either by impressing designs and words into the clay when it was still wet or by the slow process of painting words and pictures on to the partly baked clay surface by hand. Both methods were unsuitable for the era of mass production which was about to dawn; with rapidly increasing demand for all types of decorated wares potters were obliged to seek a speedier method of repeating uniform designs on their products.

The answer was found shortly before the end of the 18th century when potteries in Liverpool successfully applied designs by transfer printing. Decorations were first printed on sheets of specially prepared paper from engraved copper plates. These paper transfers were laid onto the surface of the pot at the unglazed or 'biscuit' stage, and when the paper was washed off the inks remained. The pot was then glazed and baked so that the design became an integral part of the finished article.

Coloured lids

By 1830 transfer-printed pots and jars were being used by manufacturers of snuff, toothpaste, hair preparations, fish and meat pastes, face creams and pharmaceutical ointments. The advertising which appeared on the containers was printed in black or a single colour and because the pots were often less than 3in. high it became common practice to print the design in a circular lay-out on the lid of the container. It is these transfer-printed pot lids which have become the most enthusiastically collected of all objects found in Victorian rubbish dumps.

In the 1840s one or two firms developed methods of transfer-printing in several colours. Of those companies which developed multicoloured pot lids the best known is F. and R. Pratt of Fenton, Staffordshire. Their chief engraver was Jesse

Underglaze transfers were also used on Victorian pots and jars.

Austin who worked for the company from about 1845 until his death in 1879, during which time he produced numerous engravings for pot lids which were printed in up to five colours.

Manufacturers of bear's grease, or pomatum, were probably the first to use the new multicoloured lids. Bear's grease was at that time a popular hair dressing and attractive coloured pot lids showing dancing bears and similar motifs were soon being turned out in large numbers by the Staffordshire pottery.

Another group of manufacturers who were quick to realize that a pretty coloured pot lid could be beneficial to sales were the shrimp paste makers of Pegwell Bay near Ramsgate. The shrimping trade in this village flourished between 1847 and 1875 and throughout this period local firms placed large orders for coloured lids showing views of the surrounding district and other designs. The village of Pegwell Bay was the most popular subject portrayed on the lids, while shrimpers at work, views of Ramsgate and Margate and delightful still life designs showing fishes and game were also used.

Within a few years coloured pot lids were being issued by numerous manufacturers whose wares were suitable for packaging in pots. Cold creams, shaving creams, tooth pastes, bloater and anchovy pastes, chocolate sauce and other products were sold in pots with lids depicting beautiful women, ornamental gardens, royalty, coats of arms, famous generals, buildings, scenes from Shakespeare's plays and many other subjects. The Crystal Palace was a popular subject for pot lids during and after the Great Exhibition of 1851, and events such as the Siege of Sabastopol during the Crimean War were also portrayed in glorious colours. Some of the lids bore the name and address of the manufacturer who used the pot; others included details of the pot's contents with the picture on the lid; but large numbers carried no words or symbols to indicate that they were used on commercial containers. All advertising matter, including the company's name and details of the pot's contents, were either transfer-printed on the body of the pot or printed on a paper label which wrapped around the container.

Marble-stoppered rarities: a Rylands' "Valve" Codd; an amber-brown Codd; and a pale-blue specimen with beehive top.

Embossing, shoulder seals, and beautiful glass colour make these bottles prized specimens.

A Victorian syphon in blue glass with pewter tap.

Victorian "quack" medicine bottles.

A beautiful display of inexpensive
antique bottles showing the wide
range of colours and shapes used in
the 19th century by makers of
mineral water and beer bottles.

The great coloured pot lid era drew to a close in the 1880s, mainly because multicoloured paper labels were readily available and the costs of producing coloured pot lids by transfer printing had risen considerably. They did not, however, die out altogether. Even before the end of the 19th century there were a few collectors of coloured pot lids and their numbers have steadily increased since then. To satisfy collectors' needs some lids have from time to time been reproduced from those original copper plates which have been preserved. This practice has continued to the present day.

Black and white lids

Coloured pot lids can be found in late Victorian rubbish dumps but their numbers are few because most of the dumps explored by diggers date from after 1880. The vast majority of pot lids which do come to light are those printed with black transfers on white backgrounds which were in use before coloured lids appeared and which were not superseded by paper labels until the 1890s or later. More than one thousand different black-and-white transfer designs have so far been recovered by dump diggers and most of these have come from sites in the south of England. It seems probable that this figure will double when Victorian refuse sites in other areas are fully explored.

The pot lid with which most dump diggers start their collections is Burgess's Anchovy Paste (see below). It bears a coat-of-arms and gives the company's address as 107 Strand, Corner of Savoy Steps, London. The transfer was registered as a trade mark by John Burgess & Son in July, 1876 and the company claimed use for forty years prior to that date. The

This trade mark was first used by John Burgess in 1836. It appears on the company's anchovy paste pot lids for more than 80 years with only slight modifications.

BURGESS'S,
Genuine

The Original Fish Sauce Warehouse

107 Strand corner of the Savoy steps London

DIEU ET DROIT
MON

Anchovy Paste.
for Toast Biscuit &c.

same lid bearing a Willesden address was still in use in the early years of the 20th century when the company moved to new premises in north London. A close examination of some of the Burgess lids which have been found reveal minor differences in the printed design. It is obvious that transfers were printed from several different engravings and it seems likely that a number of different potteries produced Burgess lids during the eighty or more years in which they were used. Some were probably made by F. and R. Pratt who also produced a coloured lid showing Shakespeare's birthplace for this company.

Another example which is found frequently in late Victorian dumps is an Areca Nut Tooth Paste pot lid issued by W. Woods of Plymouth. The paste was sold in sixpenny, one shilling, and one and sixpenny pots and there are several variations in the transfers used for each size. Transfer variations have been noted on many other well-known lids and these are being recorded by collectors in the hope that a comprehensive catalogue might be compiled.

The rarest black-and-white lids are those used for bear's grease which, like the coloured varieties, usually carry a picture of a chained or dancing bear. The best-known are those issued by James Atkinson of 24 Old Bond Street, London, who was packing bear's grease in pots as early as 1830. His lids show a picture of a bear wearing a muzzle; four sizes priced at 2s 6d (12½p), 3s 0d (15p) 4s 0d (20p) and 5s 0d (25p) have been found.

Tooth pastes form the largest group of transfer-printed pot lids, with cold creams and fish and meat pastes taking second and third places. Lids from pots containing shaving creams, healing ointments, confectionery, snuff and spices are included in the wide variety already recovered from Victorian dumps. The majority are round and vary in size from 2½ in. to 4½ in. in diameter; but square, oblong and even triangular lids are not unknown. A few examples with pink, blue or green transfers have also been found. No doubt more surprises await diligent diggers in the many dumps yet to be explored.

Paper bands like the one shown here were usually wrapped around the body of the pot. Circular paper labels eventually replaced under-glaze printing on the lid.

Selective price guide to black-and-white lids

This list was compiled by examining pot-lid collections owned by members of the British Bottle Collectors' Club in various parts of Britain and it includes those lids found in most large collections. To describe the lids as 'common finds' would be misleading; even Burgess lids are by no means prolific in any dump. A full day spent digging an 1890s site might produce twenty-five bottles worth keeping but it is unlikely that more than two or three pot lids would be recovered in the same time.

These lids are most likely to be found in Victorian dumps—throughout Britain because the products their pots contained were sold nationally or over a wide area of the country. There are other lids which are equally well-known, but most of them are found within limited areas covering only one or two counties.

An alphabetical pricing guide has been added to give an approximate indication of the current retail price for each lid. The prices quoted are those at which pot lids have sold during the past year and they refer to specimens in perfect condition. Lids with cracks or chips are worth considerably less. The alphabetical guide should be interpreted as follows:

A — £4.00–£6.00
B — £6.00–£10.00
C — £10.00–£15.00

Note: In the face of inflation and an ever-increasing interest in pot lid collecting, prices must continue their upward trent. If those lids in category A rise in price by 50% during the next twelve months the lids in categories B and C must do likewise, because the letters A, B, and C indicate *rarity* as well as current prices.

The advertisment shows the transfer printed lids and the paper band which was wrapped around the pot.

59

TOOTHPASTES

Wood's Areca Nut (A)
Wood's Cherry (A)
Lorimer's Areca Nut (B)
Parke's Areca Nut (B)
Parke's Cherry (B)
Cracroft's Areca Nut (A)
Timothy White's Cherry (A)
Calvert's Carbolic (A)
Army & Navy Co-op Cherry (A)
Pond's Areca Nut (A)
Hill's Eucalyptus (B)
Cleaver's Saponaceous (B)
Cleaver's Areca Nut (A)
Maw's Cherry (A)
Maw's White Cherry (A)
Maw's Indian Betal Nut (A)
Maw's White Rose (square lid) (B)
Bragg's Charcoal (oblong lid) (C)
Bristow's Cherry (oblong lid) (B)
Allen's Areca Nut and Cherry (A)
Ziemer's Alexandra (B)
Gosnell's Cherry (B)
Gosnell's Cherry (miniature; approx. 1½ in. dia.) (C)
Goss's Cherry (A)
Keene & Ashworth's Dentifrice (B)
Lewis & Burrows' Areca Nut (A)
Lewis & Burrows' Cherry (A)
Lewis & Burrows' Cherry (square lid) (B)
Dodd's Cherry (A)
Jewsbury & Brown's Oriental (A)
Darling's American Dentifrice (B)
Boots' Cherry (A)
Common's Areca Nut (A)
Robert's Areca Nut (A)
Savory & Moore's American Dentifrice (B)
Windle's Cherry Areca Nut (A)
Hodgkinson, Preston & King's Royal Cherry (oblong lid) (C)
Cook's Tooth Soap (oblong lid) (B)
Robert's Coralline (oblong lid) (C)
Saunder's Red Cherry (B)
Lockyer's Cherry (A)
T. & S. Areca Nut (B)
Prosser Roberts' Areca Nut (B)
Crown Perfumery's Cherry (B)
Cooper's Carnation (B)
Giles' Cherry (A)
Gilbertson's Cherry (A)
A.D.I. Tooth Powder (B)
Windle's Cherry (A)
Burgoyne Burbidge's Cherry (C)

COLD CREAMS

Rowland's Otto of Rose (A)
Parke's Cold Cream of Roses (A)
Parke's Otto of Rose (A)
Boots' Cold Cream (A)
Army & Navy Co-op Cold Cream of Roses (A)
Goss's Otto of Rose (A)
Junior Army & Navy Stores Cold Cream of Roses (B)
Starkie's Rose Cold Cream (B)
Atkinson's Rose Cold Cream (A)
Robert's Glycerine Cold Cream (B)
Home & Colonial Rose Cold Cream (A)
Hovenden's Creme d'Amande (B)
Universities Toilet Club Cream of Almonds (B)
Patey's Cold Cream (A)

Davis & Son's Otto of Rose (B)
Grossmith's Rose Cold Cream (A)
Rogers' Cold Cream (A)
Gosnell's Cold Cream (A)
Lorimer's Cold Cream of Roses (A)
Bayley's Cold Cream of Roses (A)
Pinaud's Cold Cream (A)
Civil Service Co-op Cold Cream (B)
Breidenbach's Cold Cream of Rose (B)
Maw's Otto of Rose (A)
White's Cold Cream (A)
Heppell's Otto of Rose (A)
Squire's Cold Cream (A)
Autard's Creme Aspasie (B)

MEAT AND FISH PASTES

Burgess's Anchovy (A)
Gilson's Cream of Bloater (A)
Keddie's Gorgona Anchovy (A)
Keddie's Bloater (A)
Fortnum & Mason's Anchovy (A)
Fortnum & Mason's Potted Beef (A)
Fortnum & Mason's Chicken and Ham (A)
Army & Navy Co-op Gorgona Anchovy (A)
Army & Navy Co-op Home Made Potted Meats (A)
Crosse & Blackwell's Anchovy (A)
Darby's Fluid Meat (B)
Harrod's Gorgona Anchovy (A)
Harrod's Bloater (A)
Morel Bros., Corbett & Sons' Anchovy (A)

SHAVING CREAMS

Jaschke's Shaving Cream (A)
Charles' Shaving Cream (A)
Army & Navy Co-op Almond Shaving Cream (A)
Viane's Shaving Cream (A)
Price's Prince Albert Shaving Cream (B)
Mitchell & Eden's Shaving Cream (A)
Maw's Ambrosial Shaving Cream (B)
Blondeau's Vinolia Shaving Cream (B)
Army & Navy Toilet Club's United Service Shaving Cream (C)
London Soap and Candle Company's Ambrosial Shaving Cream (B)

POMADES AND BEAR'S GREASE

Atkinson's Bear's Grease (C)
Cleaver's Bear's Grease (B)
Boehm's Anti-Scurf Pomade (B)
Curtis's Pomade (B)
Letherby's Logwood Pomade (B)
Lewis's Skin Pomade (B)

HEALING OINTMENTS

Mrs Ellen Hale's Heal-all Ointment (B)
Holloway's Ointment (B)

CONFECTIONERY

Buzard's Bride Cake (B)

6 Clay tobacco pipes

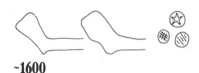

~1600

Stems: 3-4 inches. *Marks:* very rare. A few have simple marks incised on the spur beneath the bowl as in the example shown.

1600~1650

Stems: 7-8 inches. *Marks:* scarce. Some have simple marks or maker's initials incised on the spur beneath the bowl. (a) West Country type.

Clay tobacco pipes were first made in England during the late 16th century when merchant adventurers who voyaged to the New World brought home cargoes of tobacco from the West Indies. Kaolin, or pipe clay as it soon became known, was already used by potters in Bristol and Shropshire for making slipware and moulded figurines and it proved an ideal material for imitating the wooden pipes which sailors had seen in the Caribbean. Within a few years a number of potteries in these areas were turning out small batches of tiny pipes with bowls less than 1in. deep which were passed around between groups of smokers, who shared the cost of filling the bowl because at that time tobacco was priced at the present-day equivalent of £10.00 an ounce.

In spite of its expense the smoking habit persisted. The Company and Craft of Tobacco Pipe Makers was incorporated in 1619 and by the end of the 17th century most large towns had pipe-makers. Important manufacturing centres at this time included Bristol, Broseley, London, Chester, Canterbury, Hull, Salisbury, York, Lynn and Selby. For the next two hundred years factories in these towns and numerous smaller makers in towns and villages throughout the country made millions of clay tobacco pipes in a rich variety of shapes and sizes which were determined by changing fashions and the fluctuating price of tobacco. The industry lasted until the 1890s by which time the popularity of cigarettes and briar pipes had put most of the makers out of business. One or two lingered on into the 20th century to earn a meagre living selling their wares in country districts or as 'curiosities' in gift shops, but save for the reproductions which have appeared recently in tobacconists' shops and on antique stalls the age of the clay tobacco pipe has passed.

Throughout its long history the industry never became

mechanized. Pipes were made by hand in simple two-piece iron moulds with which a skilled maker could produce five hundred pipes a day. A plug of wet pipe clay was placed in the mould and the bowl was formed by pressing a conical plunger into the open end. Another piece of clay was rolled around a length of wire to make the stem and the two pieces were then joined together with slip. When the clay had partially dried the wire was withdrawn and the mould opened so that the pipe could be hand-finished by scraping to remove mould marks and minor imperfections. Some makers added a touch of red or green glaze to the mouthpiece at this stage to overcome the unpleasant feel of dry clay on the lips. The pipe was then ready for firing in a moderately hot kiln which ensured a soft and porous body and a cool and pleasant smoke. In 1850 the wholesale price of pipes made in this way was 1s 6d (7½p) per gross; the retail price of each pipe was one farthing.

Sites

Riverside foreshores and Victorian rubbish dumps are the best sites on which to hunt for clay tobacco pipes. The tidal reaches of most important rivers provide a rich harvest of pipes dating from the 17th, 18th and 19th centuries, while late Victorian dumps hold large numbers of richly decorated examples from that period. Most beginners start their collections by 'mudlarking' for the early but rather plain bowls which can be picked up without much effort on riversides at low tide. More experienced collectors dip deeply into old rubbish dumps to recover ornate examples with bowls in the shape of human heads, animals and other fascinating designs which were popular towards the end of the clay tobacco pipe era. Almost all of the pipes found on riversides and many of those in dumps have broken stems, but these are easily repaired with cold-hardening modelling clays which soon restore finds to their original forms.

Dating

Only a handful of makers put dates on the pipes they made, but it is possible to date a find to within fifty years by the size of its bowl and the position of the bowl in relation to the stem. The general trend in bowl sizes was from small to large; pipes with bowls less than 1in. deep were common before 1650; between 1650 and 1700 they were made progressively larger and reached 2in. around 1800. After 1800 they were made much wider than in the last two centuries and from 1840 onwards they were reduced in depth. The exceptions to this rule were those pipes made in the west country which were generally smaller than those made elsewhere throughout the 17th and 18th centuries.

Late 16th- and early 17th-century pipes had bowls which sloped forward from the stem. In the 17th and 18th centuries bowls were gradually positioned closer to vertical in relation to

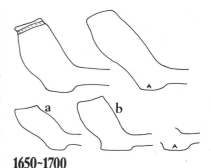

1650~1700

Stems: 8-9 inches. A few had stems up to 12 inches long. *Marks:* some have initials moulded in raised letters on the spur beneath bowl, as shown, a few have initials moulded in raised letters on either side of base of bowl, as shown on the right. (a) West Country type (b) Broseley, Shropshire type.

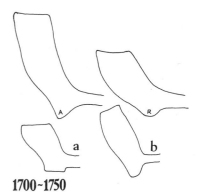

1700~1750

Stems: 16-18 inches. *Marks:* some have initials moulded in raised letters on either side of bowl. (a) West Country type (b) Imported Dutch type.

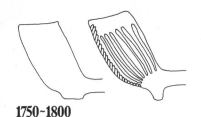

1750~1800

Stems: 24-36 inches. *Marks:* very rare. *Decoration:* a few have decorated bowls with simple designs such as ribbing around bowl or ears of corn on front or rear of bowl.

1800~1850

Stems: 24-36 inches and 8-9 inches. *Marks:* some have initials moulded in raised letters on either side of base of bowl while some have circular marks including initials incised on side of bowl. *Decoration:* Some have bowls decorated with raised designs including flowers and coats of arms. On some the decoration extends to the bowl and might include maker's address.

the stem and this trend continued throughout the 19th century until the modern 'briar pipe' shape was evolved in the 1860s.

The length of pipe stems also changed during three centuries of pipe-making. Early pipes had short stems less than 4 in. long, but 17th-century fashion decreed a length of 7 or 8 in. A pipe known as the 'Alderman' became popular at the very end of the 17th-century. This had a 12 in. stem which had increased to 16 in. by 1820. At about that time the first 'Churchwarden' pipes appeared. They had extravagent stems 2 or 3 ft in length and were popular with upper-class gentlemen until 1850. The 'Cutty', a pipe with a 7 in. stem, was a firm favourite of the 19th-century working classes.

More accurate dating of a find is sometimes possible by a close examination of markings on the pipe. Some early types have makers' marks incised, or cut, beneath the bowl, while many 18th-century pipes have the maker's initials moulded in raised, or embossed, letters on either side of a short spur on the bottom of the bowl. The initials are read correctly by holding the pipe in its smoking position with the bowl in the hand and the stem pointing towards the lips. In this position the initial on the left is that of the Christian name and the surname initial is on the right. Lists of 18th-century pipe makers have been compiled from parish registers and other sources; although they are incomplete they can help to date many pipes to within a decade or so.

The custom of placing initials on pipes died out at the end of the 18th century, though some mid-19th century makers revived the practice. After 1850 a few makers embossed or incised their full names, and occasionally their addresses, along the pipe stem. Another method of marking pipes which was used during the 17th and 18th centuries was that of moulding or impressing a design or shape known as a 'rebus' which could also be recognized as the name of the maker. Thus a family of pipe-makers called Gauntlett moulded a glove or gauntlet on the bowls of their pipes. Another maker called Bolton used a crossbow bolt piercing a barrel or tun to mark his products. The practice of making the entire bowl of the pipe in the form of a rebus was later adopted by many 19th-century public houses which purchased supplies of pipes for their customers direct from the pipe-maker. A public house called 'The Bunch of Grapes' would have pipes made with bowls shaped like bunches of grapes; another called 'The Bull' would have its pipes made with bowls in the shape of a bull's head.

In the late 19th century almost all pipe bowls were decorated. Coats-of-arms, heads of politicians, members of the Royal Family, famous generals, music hall celebrities, and many other public figures and unusual objects appeared on pipe bowls. Most of those which are found come from rubbish dumps and they are easily dated to within a few years by checking records of refuse disposal on the sites where they are recovered.

The illustrations and notes which follow are a guide to *approximate* dating. The line drawings show typical bowl shapes of the period to which they refer, but it should be noted that there were many deviations from the norm in bowl shape, bowl size, stem length and methods of marking.

Pipe prices

Complete pipes with unbroken, unrepaired stems are relentlessly pursued by collectors. Approximate prices fetched for such specimens are laid out below. Any increase in price over the next few years will be proportionate within these groups.

Plain bowls, short stems	up to £2.00
Plain bowls, long stems	up to £5.00
Decorated bowls	£1.00—£3.00
Figurehead bowls	£3.00—£5.00
Large figurehead bowls	£5.00—£10.00

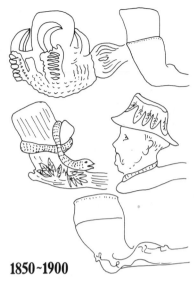

1850~1900

Stems: 4-9 inches. *Marks:* initials are rare. Full names are often found on stems or bowls. Bowls might be a rebus for maker's name, public house, etc. *Decoration:* the majority of bowls are decorated; some very simply, others elaborately. Bowls are often fashioned as human or animal heads, claws etc. Masonic pipes are common. Spurs are often moulded in shape of a shoe, ball, etc. Pipes with extra large bowls sometimes found.

7 Other finds

Glass and ceramics

Although commercial containers such as lemonade and beer bottles, ink and blacking pots and printed pot lids make up the bulk of those glass and ceramic objects found in old rubbish dumps, a rich variety of plates, cups, teapots, vases, ornaments and similar household objects can also be found. Many are cracked, chipped or broken when recovered because they were thrown away for those reasons; but repairs are often possible and an otherwise worthless object can sometimes be transformed into a collector's item with a little care and patience. Egg-cups and lids from teapots and storage jars are usually found undamaged. They were thrown away for different reasons—because others in a set were broken, or because the container to which the lid fitted was damaged—and, being small, they survive intact to form interesting and unusual collections for many diggers.

Repairable pottery from a Victorian dump.

A vase, a shaving mug, a bird-on-a-branch—worth digging up and worth collecting.

Pottery found in 19th-century dumps is usually of Victorian manufacture, but earlier finds are sometimes made. I know of one digger who found a headless porcelain figure which an expert identified as having been made by the Derby Porcelain Factory in the 1760s. One year later, while working on the same dump, the digger found the head of the piece. He is now the proud owner of a repaired but valuable antique. Dump diggers refer to such finds as 'old when thrown' and anyone excavating a Victorian dump should be on the look-out for them. If you suspect any object you find of being considerably older than other items recovered from a site take it to a reputable antique dealer specializing in pottery and porcelain.

Heads and limbs from Victorian dolls are fairly common finds in 19th-century dumps. Many of the heads have impressed pottery marks and dates which indicate they were made in Germany between 1880 and 1900. They and the many arms and legs which are found come from dolls which had soft bodies made from wood or cloth which do not survive in dumps. For the same reason large numbers of glass, jet and other non-metallic buttons are found; they were probably attached to articles of clothing when thrown away.

Rubbish dumps being what they are, almost anything can turn up on the end of your fork. Glass stoppers from decanters, colourful tiles from Victorian fireplaces and walls, cooking utensils, plaques and chamber pots are some of the items which can be collected by diligent digging. All glass and ceramic objects which are undamaged, or nearly so, should be salvaged. You will soon meet a digger whose interests extend to some of the objects you find and who will be pleased to 'trade' if you do not intend to make your own collection of these items.

67

More dump finds.

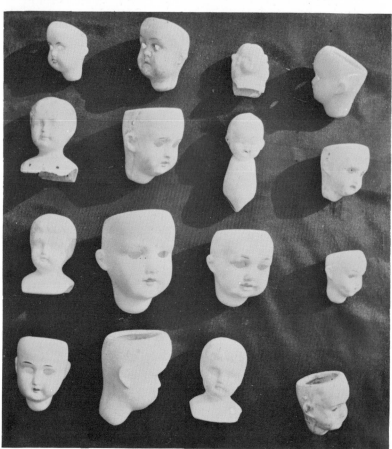

A selection of doll's heads recovered from a dump in Buckinghamshire.

68

Metal objects

Coins are undoubtedly the commonest metal objects found on tidal riversides. They can date from any period from pre-Roman to modern and they are easily identified with the aid of a numismatic catalogue. Tokens, which might be described as private coinage, were once widely used as substitutes for legal tender and tidal riversides are usually littered with them. Many date from the 17th and 18th centuries when there was a great shortage of low-denomination coinage. Merchants resolved the problem by issuing copper tokens which carried their names and addresses and which could be used in place of pennies, halfpennies and farthings. Inn keepers and small traders also issued tokens which were usually made from lead. Some were stamped with names or initials, others with public house signs. Those which were not melted down when legal coinage became more readily available were thrown away and large numbers found their way into rivers.

Metal buttons and buckles form the second largest group of riverside relics. Undecorated lead buttons are usually the first finds made by newcomers to mudlarking. They vary in size form ½ in. to 2 in. in diameter and they have two holes at the centre. Some have been dated to the Roman period, but they were also in wide use in the 19th century when they were sewn into the hems of ladies' skirts to ensure neat hemlines. Brass and pewter buttons were also used for several hundred years on both civilian and military dress. Those dating from the 16th and 17th centuries were often elaborately decorated, while Victorian examples usually carried a maker's name. Brass and copper buckles were generally less elaborate, though silver shoe buckles from the 17th and 18th centuries were often richly ornamented.

Medieval pilgrims' badges have already been mentioned as possible riverside finds. They are far less common than the numerous military badges which litter most riversides and which tell their own story of Britain's long and glorious military history. Badges from almost every regiment which served on the frontiers of our 19th-century empire can be recovered from the foreshores of rivers used by returning troops, who seem to have made a habit of throwing badges into rivers as they left their ships. Uniformed members of police forces, fire brigades, omnibus companies and similar organizations were equally careless with their insignia.

The millions of tons of exported goods which have been shipped from Britain's ports during the past several hundred years have left a rich legacy of riverside relics in the shape of lead tallies once used to mark bales of cloth and other packages bound for overseas markets. These tallies are usually circular and have small tongues by which they were attached to the containers they identified. Each tally was marked by squeezing

Coins discovered in various parts of the country.

69

More old coins found by dump-diggers.

it in a pair of pincers which impressed letters, a name, a date or a coat-of-arms into the lead. The earliest examples found date from the Tudor period, though 17th- and 18th-century tallies are more common.

Keys, musketballs, pins, fishing weights, Victorian metal toys, antique jewellery, weapons—a list of likely finds on any tidal riverside must include these and many more metal relics. The only prediction which can be made with certainty is that the next falling tide is sure to reveal objects worth collecting. If you search the foreshore of your local river for several days and pick up all interesting metal objects which catch your eye, and if you then compare your collection with those river-found relics displayed in the local museum, you will learn much about the finds you have made and the finds you are likely to make if you concentrate your mudlarking activities on that river.

8 Picture gallery

Dan Rylands' 'Valve' bottle

Dan Rylands' 'Valve' was first patented in 1887 and it marks the peak of development in globe-stoppered mineral water bottles. It was developed to overcome the problem of the bottle's contents spurting from the mouth when the glass marble was pressed downwards with the wooden opener used on standard globe-stoppered bottles. On the 'Valve' model gas pressure was released by pressing the small glass plunger in the shoulder. This operation opened an india-rubber valve which allowed gas to escape until the marble dropped from its 'closed' position in the mouth.

Although it was an extremely efficient globe-stoppered bottle, the 'Valve' failed to achieve widespread popularity with the mineral water trade because of its relatively high cost. It was the most expensive mineral water bottle made by Dan Rylands and he made strenuous efforts to persuade mineral water makers to adopt it; but digging evidence shows that only a handful of companies were prepared to risk high-cost bottles to save their customers the inconvenience of spurting lemonade.

This particular example, made for Talbot & Co of Gloucester, is a most interesting find. Two eyes have been embossed on the shoulder above the glass plunger to create a smiling face. Talbot registered this device as a trade mark—an indication of the company's pride in their new bottles!

The specimen was recovered from cellars beneath a Victorian public house being demolished as part of a road-widening scheme. The finder arrived on the site to find workmen using the old bottles they had removed from the building as targets in a stone-throwing game. This was the only specimen to escape destruction. Such stories are common in bottle-collecting circles and more often than not blame for the destruction will be heaped upon the workmen who break the bottles. Further investigation often reveals that an opportunity to search the building before the demolition contractor started work was missed by the collector. No building is ever demolished on the day the occupiers move out; often entire streets of shops and public houses remain unoccupied for several months before they are pulled down. A polite request for permission to carry out a search made to the local council, the building contractor or the demolition gang working in the next street as soon as possible after the building is abandoned by its occupiers will save many bottles and other relics from destruction.

Sykes-Macvay bottle of 1877

A Sykes-Macvay patent of 1877, this internally stoppered bottle has six indents at the bottom of the bottle which trapped the marble after it was pushed from its 'closed' position in the neck. Like Dan Rylands, Sykes and Macvay established their glassworks in Yorkshire (Castleford) and sold their bottle throughout Britain. Although they never achieved the output of Rylands' glassworks at Barnsley their bottles enjoyed brief popularity in the Midlands, Wales and Cornwall.

They had two disadvantages which contributed to their eventual disappearance from the mineral water scene: firstly, the india-rubber washer in the neck was held in position by a collar of lead (or a lead alloy) which must have raised serious doubts about the bottle's suitability as a container for mineral waters when the causes of lead poisoning were investigated in the 1890s. Secondly, because the marble fell from the neck of the bottle to the base on opening, and because it was able to move about freely inside the bottle after the contents had been poured, internal chipping and cracks on the bottle's inner surfaces were common. This reduced the working life of each bottle and increased costs for the mineral water maker.

This last disadvantage should be noted by collectors. When you find or buy any internally stoppered bottle within which the stopper moves freely examine the inside of the bottle as carefully as you check the outer surfaces for cracks and chips which considerably reduce a bottle's value.

This specimen was found near Castleford, Yorkshire on a site near the old glassworks. Such dumps are always worth close inspection. They are most likely to contain large numbers of bottles made at the nearby works and it is sometimes possible to find extremely rare examples of bottles which were made as experiments but which never went into large-scale production.

Barrett and Elers bottle *c.* 1871

The Barrett and Elers bottle which went into production after 1871. The original stopper covered in the patent of that year consisted of a hollow wooden plug into which a wooden valve was inserted. The production version was much simpler—a solid plug with a large india-rubber washer firmly held at the lower end which formed a gas-tight seal against the sloping shoulders of the bottle. The wood from which the stopper was made had a greater specific gravity than water and it sank slowly to the bottom of the bottle when gas pressure was released by pushing the plug downwards. Like many other internally stoppered bottles it often spurted some of its contents when it was opened.

This bottle was the great rival of Hiram Codd's globe-stoppered invention which arrived on the scene one year later. Within those twelve months Barrett and Elers had captured a large market for their new bottle and they mounted an impressive advertising campaign in mineral water trade journals to maintain their sales for several years. The main cause of their failure to compete with Codd in the long term was Ben Rylands' success at making globe-stoppered bottles on a large scale and to a high standard in strength of glass and accuracy in moulding.

Examples of Barrett and Elers' bottles are difficult to find even though large numbers were made. You must look for a site holding refuse which was dumped before 1885 to be reasonably sure of finding specimens. Any dump which has fragments of Barrett and Elers bottles on its surface is likely to hold rich rewards for those who dig it deeply and efficiently. This example came from a dump in County Durham being excavated to recover ash for a motorway construction project. It was found twenty feet from the surface and it came out on the end of a mechanical shovel. Permission to search the extracted ash was obtained from the contractor.

Sealed bottles had fallen in popularity by the time of large-scale dumping which occurred in Britain during the late 19th century. Those which are found are most likely to be of foreign manufacture like the examples shown here. The specimen on the left is a liqueur, the one on the right is a rum bottle. The circumstances under which they were found are interesting.

On the banks of the Grand Union Canal in Buckinghamshire is a large Victorian dump known to hundreds of bottle collectors in south-east England. It occupies a one-acre site on the canal side adjacent to the confluence of the main canal and a branch canal which once served towns in the west of the county. Its exact location was pin-pointed by research into London's refuse disposal methods in the 1890s, by talking to old people who had lived and worked on the canal at the turn of the century and finally by walking the canal banks to find a spot where large refuse barges would have been able to manoeuvre without preventing free movement of other traffic along the busy main canal when unloading their cargoes.

After its discovery the site was methodically dug to a depth of five feet at which a clay bottom was reached. Thousands of excellent finds were made during the next two years by all who dug there; few collections in the London area do not include bottles, pipes and pot lids from this 'bonanza' and bottle collectors from many parts of Britain, the United States and Canada also declared the site to be one of the best they had ever visited. When these highly productive days came to an end several months ago a small group of local diggers decided to attempt one last deep excavation. They were helped by a friendly civil engineering contractor who was working near the site at the time and who removed many cubic yards of ashes to expose a wide area of clay bottom. The bottle collectors then continued to dig through this unproductive clay for a further three feet. At that depth a new seam of ash was revealed and it took less than half an hour to confirm the presence of a second and much older dump beneath the clay. It is from this layer that the two sealed bottles shown here were recovered.

Later research indicated that during the digging of the main canal clay was taken from land flanking its course to 'puddle' the bottom and make it impervious to water. The resulting clay pits were used as refuse dumps by London boroughs after 1870 and it was at about this time that a large gravel pit was first opened close to the site on which these two sealed bottles were found. Overlying clay from the gravel workings was also thrown into the rubbish dump and this clay covered the dump's contents to a depth of three feet. More London refuse was later dumped on top of the clay to provide this marvellous site.

79

'Black' glass beer bottles

'Black' glass beer bottles like those shown here are always found to be dark brown or dark green when held up to strong light. The glass was coloured by adding iron oxide during manufacture, but it was never possible to produce true black glass.

The bottles in the photograph show the evolution of beer bottle shapes from 1850 to 1900. The example on the left does not have a seal and it is unembossed, but the width of its body and neck are typical of beer bottles made in the mid-19th century. This bottle had a cork stopper; its wide and hand-finished lip was necessary in order to hold the wires or strings used to secure the cork. Prior to 1870 the wiring of corks was done by hand.

The sealed bottle (centre) was probably made in the early 1880s. Its shape is much more symmetrical than the bottle on the left which indicates that it was more accurately moulded. The lip is also machine-made to accurate dimensions and although this bottle was also stoppered by a wired cork this operation too was probably done by a machine.

Screw stoppers made from ebonite and having an india-rubber washer which formed an efficient gas seal when the stopper was tightened were used on beer bottles from the 1880s until quite recent times. The crown cap used on most beer bottles nowadays began its rise to popularity in 1903, but it was not widely used until the 1930s. The screw-stoppered bottle on the right is dated by its embossing. Gomm & Son of Brentford ceased to trade in 1905.

All three bottles were found in or near the Thames. The one on the left was dug out of the Thames' mud near Blackfriars Bridge; the sealed bottle and the screw-stoppered specimen were found in a silted creek on the Essex marshes once used by refuse barges carrying rubbish from the City.

Irish whiskey jar

This Irish whiskey jar was found by a bottle collector in New Zealand where the hobby has a large following. It was excavated from the foundations of a waterfront hotel in Wellington which was demolished as part of a harbour improvement scheme. The hotel was a wooden building resting on heavy timber piles and the space beneath its lower floor had been used as a dump for hotel refuse.

Earthenware containers were commonly used for exports of beer, spirits and other liquids in the 19th century. They were much stronger than glass bottles and they were often subject to less customs duty. Thousands of shiploads left British ports every year for our Empire outposts and overseas markets and they eventually found their way to rubbish dumps in those countries.

This particular find happened to duplicate a jar already in the New Zealander's collection so he traded it for several clay tobacco pipes with a British collector. Because the hobby is international, with thousands of enthusiasts in the United States, Canada, Britain, Australia, New Zealand and South Africa, many such transactions take place. Fortunately these countries have a common language and efficient postal systems in addition to similar 19th-century bottle histories. It is therefore very easy to send finds, historical information, letters, magazines and books between one country and another.

82

Cobalt blue poison bottles

Poison bottles in cobalt blue glass. Although the bottle on the left was identified by its colour as a bottle which contained a poisonous substance it could not be recognized at night in a poorly lit bedroom. The bottle next to it is of triangular shape and it has embossed projections on its surfaces. It is therefore easily identified by touch. Such bottles came into general use in the 1880s (though the idea was patented thirty years earlier). A further advantage claimed by chemists who used them was that their triangular base reduced the chance of accidental spillage.

The two bottles on the right have embossed vertical lines on their sides—another method of identifying poison bottles widely used in the late 19th century. These two examples held two fluid ounces; most collectors attempt to build complete sets in ½ oz, 1 oz, 2 oz, 4 oz, 6 oz, 8 oz, 16 oz and 20 oz capacities.

Cobalt blue poison bottles are found in all Victorian dumps, but perfect specimens are difficult to obtain. The blue glass is readily attacked by acids in rubbish dumps which coat it with a white deposit known to collectors and diggers as 'sickness'. It cannot be removed by cleaning, though it is possible to disguise it by painting the bottle with clear resin or varnish. Bottles so treated are worth considerably less than perfect specimens.

Warner's 'Safe' Cure

A Warner's 'Safe' Cure in dark green glass found in a dump near an abandoned lead mine in Yorkshire. After eighty years in the ground it proved to be in perfect condition when accumulated dirt was washed away—no cracks or chips around the lip, glass unpitted by acids in the dump, embossing deeply and evenly moulded. Such qualities must always be assessed in bottles dug out of the ground. Beginners often make the mistake of carrying home every object they excavate from a site only to find, when they learn more about the hobby, that most of their collections must be relegated to the dustbin because the bottles are clouded by acid attack on the glass or because a specimen is cracked and chipped. A collection of ten perfect bottles looks far better when displayed and is worth considerably more than a collection of one hundred 'sick' specimens which should rightly have been left in the dump. Strive for quality not quantity and your bottles will increase in value and give greater satisfaction as a collection.

Readers who find examples of Dr Warner's bottles should note that there are several varieties. The bottle in the photograph came in two sizes priced at 4s 6d (22½p) and 2s 9d (14p) per bottle; there are dark green and light brown varieties of both. Warner also produced 'Safe' Nervine and 'Safe' Diabetes cures which have those words embossed on their respective bottles. Overseas readers will find examples with the words TORONTO, MELBOURNE, ROCHESTER (U.S.A.), and FRANKFURT embossed where the example in the photograph has LONDON.

POISONOUS
PLYNINE Coy
LTD
EDINBURGH
HOUSEHOLD AMMONIA

Earthenware ammonia bottle

Many surprises await those bottle collectors who dig the thousands of unexcavated Victorian refuse sites that await discovery in northern England, Scotland, Wales and Ireland. This is confirmed by an unusual bottle from a dump near Edinburgh. Until it was found by a British Bottle Collectors' Club member from Fifeshire the club's files on recovered bottles did not include reference to the use of transfer-printed earthenware bottles for poisonous liquids. Those which have already been found were used for whisky, ginger beer or vinegar.

This particular bottle was obviously designed by someone who had considered the needs of the Victorian housewife or kitchen maid. It contained ammonia and was likely to have been used by someone with wet hands doing housework. In order to lessen the possibility of accidental spillage the lower part of the bottle was left unglazed and its surface roughened to provide a secure grip.

The site of the find was a long-abandoned brickworks mentioned in 19th-century Edinburgh newspapers. The location of the works was checked on a modern Ordnance Survey map which showed the site as derelict land. A visit to the area revealed the remains of old brick kilns and a trial dig on nearby land located the spot where Victorian refuse used in the brick-making process had been dumped.

89

Earthenware food jar

Earthenware jars for fish and meat pastes are scarce in late Victorian dumps as by that time most of these products were packaged in shallow pots with wide lids. The few companies which continued to use earthenware jars for food after 1880 attracted customers with underglaze transfer-printed jars showing views of famous buildings or events. The 'Warwick Castle' example shown here was recovered from a disused gravel pit that served as a rubbish dump before 1895. The old pit had been only partly filled with refuse and surface drainage had long ago turned it into a pond. During the particularly hot summer of 1973 this pond dried out to make possible a thorough search of its bottom which, until then, could only be searched by divers or scraped with long rakes by bottle hunters working from the water's edge.

Unusual weather conditions such as droughts and floods can help to locate good bottle-collecting and relic-hunting sites. Dried out ponds and the banks of rivers exposed when the water level is exceptionally low often reveal fragments of broken glass and pipe stem. In ponds these finds can indicate the earlier use of a gravel pit as a dump; in rivers they are often found at points where refuse barges loaded or unloaded their cargoes. Floods in rivers occasionally tear away parts of the banks to expose sites that might otherwise have been missed.

90

WARWICK CASTLE

Transfer-printed pot lids

The underglaze transfer-printed pot lids illustrated on the next few pages were all recovered from rubbish dumps. Diligent digging on any Victorian dump should produce two or three specimens for a full day's work, but they are uncommon finds in dumps dating from after 1910. If you wish to make a collection of printed pot lids you must dig on the oldest site you can locate by research and other methods. An exploratory dig on such a site should reveal decorated pipe bowls and fragments of Hamilton bottles—both probable finds in a dump likely to hold a good selection of lids. Plain (unprinted) lids are more frequently found in late dumps. When thrown away they had paper labels but these do not survive beneath the ground for more than a few years.

Products sold in pots with printed lids were luxury items bought by middle-and upper-class households. This fact can be put to good use when hunting pot lid sites in and around large towns and cities where several dumps were probably used at the same time. If you can establish which of these sites were used for rubbish collected from better-off households you will greatly increase your chances of finding printed pot lids. Dumps used for refuse collected from the west side of most cities are likely to contain the best finds because it is on the west side that wealthier citizens usually have their homes. Readers who live in seaside resorts popular in the late Victorian period should attempt to locate dumps used by large hotels in the town.

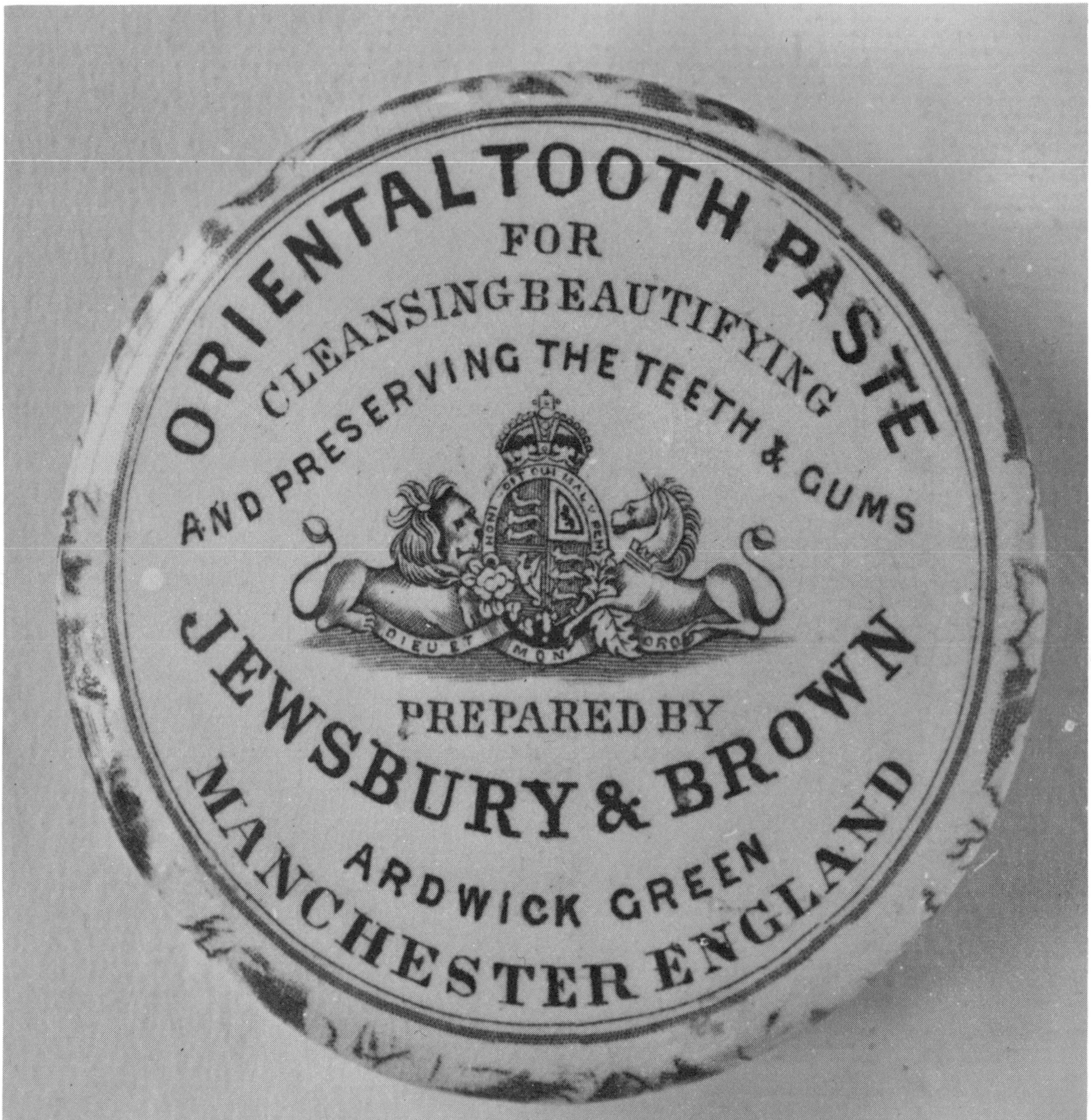
ORIENTAL TOOTH PASTE
FOR
CLEANSING BEAUTIFYING
AND PRESERVING THE TEETH & GUMS
HONI SOIT QUI MAL Y PENSE
DIEU ET MON DROIT
PREPARED BY
JEWSBURY & BROWN
ARDWICK GREEN
MANCHESTER ENGLAND

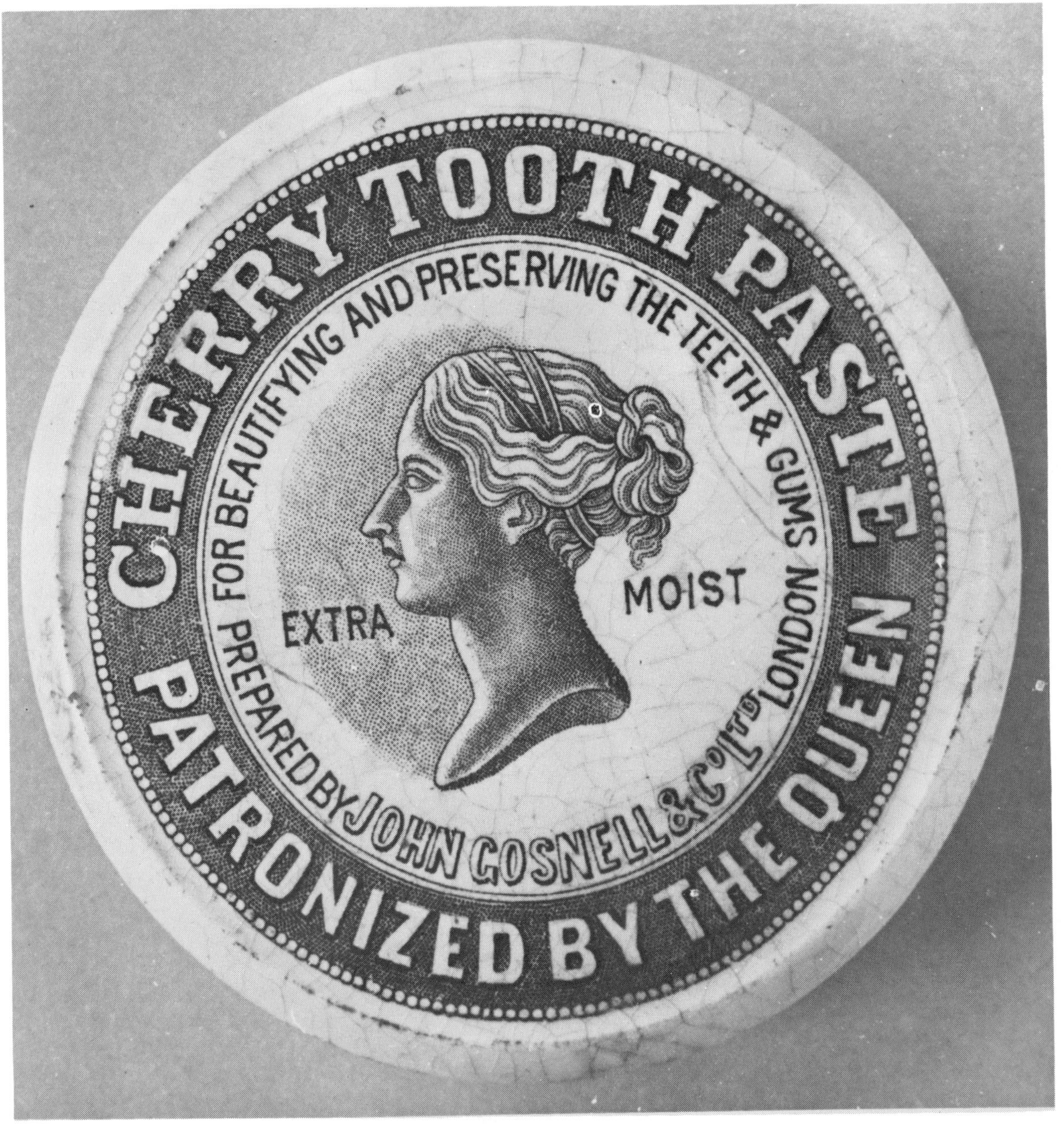
CHERRY TOOTH PASTE
FOR BEAUTIFYING AND PRESERVING THE TEETH & GUMS
EXTRA
MOIST
PREPARED BY JOHN GOSNELL & C° L^TD LONDON
PATRONIZED BY THE QUEEN

Pipes with 'head' bowls

Pipes with bowls moulded as heads are highly prized by collectors. Large examples such as the Jacob pipe shown here were often made with detachable stems so that if the stem was damaged a replacement could be fitted. This gave the pipe a much longer working life than a pipe moulded in one piece which had to be thrown away if the fragile stem was broken. A very high breakage rate is indicated by the numerous bowls found in pre-1900 dumps.

The Jacob pipe was made by Gambier of Paris, a famous manufacturer whose pipes were always elaborately decorated. They sold throughout Europe in the late 19th century and the Gambier factory continued production until the 1920s. The other pipes shown here were made in Lancashire.

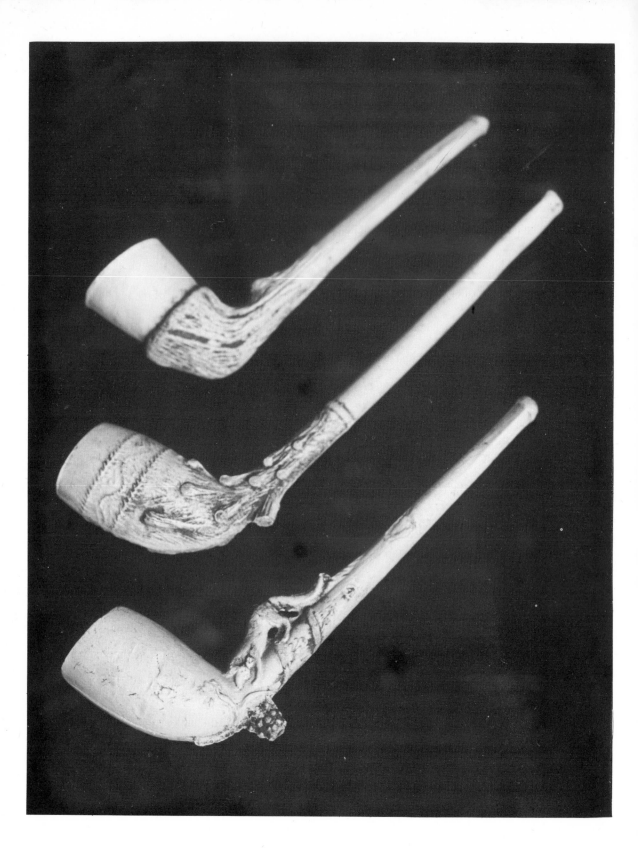

Relief-moulded clay pipes

Several thousand different decorations were used on clay tobacco pipes made between 1870 and 1900. Bowls were formed in a variety of shapes including human and animal heads, plants, fishes and inanimate objects such as buildings and items of furniture. Even a horse's hoof could inspire a maker of pipe moulds; the bowl at the top in this photograph was very popular in the days before the horseless carriage.

Relief moulding was also used to decorate pipes (centre) and such designs often covered part of the stem. Leaves and branches were much used subjects and there was keen competition between makers to produce the most artistic designs.

If a Victorian husband returned home late on Saturday night with a smell of 'the demon drink' on his breath his wife could often discover where he had spent his time by looking at the pipe in his pocket. The example at the bottom of this photograph was made for a public house called 'The Fox and Grapes'. A customer who bought his tobacco there would have been given a free pipe in which to smoke it as he stood at the bar drinking the landlord's ale. Most public houses used this form of advertising a hundred years ago and dumps containing large amounts of refuse taken from Victorian ale houses are always rich in pipe finds.

'Santa Claus' pipe bowl

This 'Santa Claus' pipe bowl is 4 in. tall; and more than 3 oz of tobacco are required to fill the bowl. It is an example of those late Victorian pipes made for communal smoking in masonic lodges, gentlemen's clubs and other places where men gathered for business and pleasure and where a pipe of tobacco was passed around among those present. Santa Claus was a popular subject for these large pipes and this suggests that many all-male gatherings took place around Christmastide.

This example was found by a diver in the Thames near Reading. In the upper reaches of the river visibility is sufficiently good to make underwater searches beneath bridges and near mooring and docking points highly profitable for the amateur treasure hunter equipped with diving gear and having the necessary qualifications. Those who do not possess a thorough knowledge of river diving techniques must confine their activities to areas close to the banks which can be searched with a glass-bottomed bucket and a river rake when the water level is low.

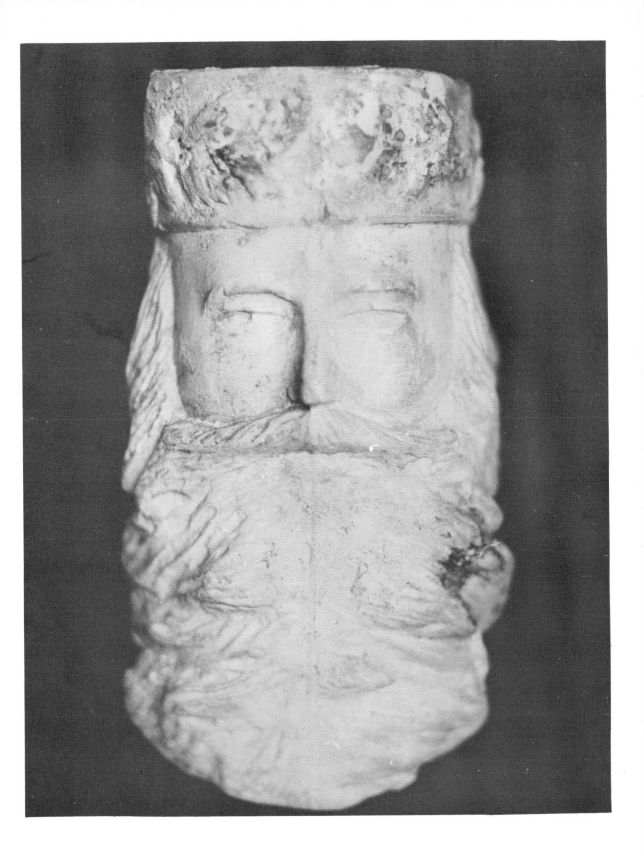

China figures

The boy with a boat was headless when he turned up on the end of a digging fork during a group 'dig' organized by the Essex branch of the British Bottle Collectors' Club on the site of a Victorian dump owned by Southend Corporation. The club member who found him was sufficiently experienced to know that the various parts of a broken piece of pottery or china which were placed in a dustbin one hundred years ago are very likely to lie close together in the dump into which the dustbin's contents were eventually thrown. This was proved when the digger found the head one hour later less than a yard from the spot where he dug up the body. The repaired statue, which has a Bristol pottery mark, made an attractive addition to his collection.

The girl with the basket of fruit also had a piece missing when she was found; part of the base of the figure was broken. The finder recovered her from the bottom of a canal which flanked a Victorian dump on the outskirts of Leeds. He used a long-handled rake which he dragged back and forth across the canal bottom close to a derelict mooring point once used by refuse barges. Although several pot lids and bottles were recovered by this method the small piece missing from the base of the statue was not found. Nevertheless, it was possible to make good the damage using a resin-based pottery repair material.

Boy doll's head

A doll's head from a dump in Kent. It is 1½ in. high with hand-painted blue eyes and a brown moustache. Incised pottery marks on the base of the neck indicate it was made in Germany in 1883, probably for a doll dressed in a soldier's uniform. It is a rarity in gender only; most heads recovered from Victorian dumps are from female dolls. They vary in size from 1 in. to 4 in. and almost all are of German origin. Digging evidence suggests the smaller heads are older; 3 in. and 4 in. heads are far more common in early 20th-century dumps. Legs and arms are also found and most diggers aim to collect matched sets—two arms, two legs, and a head—in the hope of having a complete reproduction doll made with original head and limbs.

Diggers fortunate in finding an early dump which contains many small heads and limbs face the problem of recovering them from the layers of ash in which they are buried. They are difficult to see when coated with fine ash and it is usually necessary to sieve the dump material to extract them. A garden sieve can be used, but better results are achieved by constructing a 'rocker'. Obtain 1 sq. yd of ½ in. wire netting and nail it to a wooden frame of the same dimensions made from 1 in. square softwood. Two ½ in. boards measuring 36 in. x 12 in. are then nailed to opposite ends of the frame. The ends of the boards which rest on the ground are cut to roughly semi-circular shape so that the frame can be rocked by pushing it with the hands.

To avoid unnecessary work when using the 'rocker' do not attempt to sieve the material you remove from a trench as you dig it out. Remove only large objects such as bottles and pot lids at this stage. When you re-fill your hole place the sieve across it and throw the loose material back into the hole through the meshes. This will trap dolls' heads, clay tobacco pipes, buttons and other small objects.

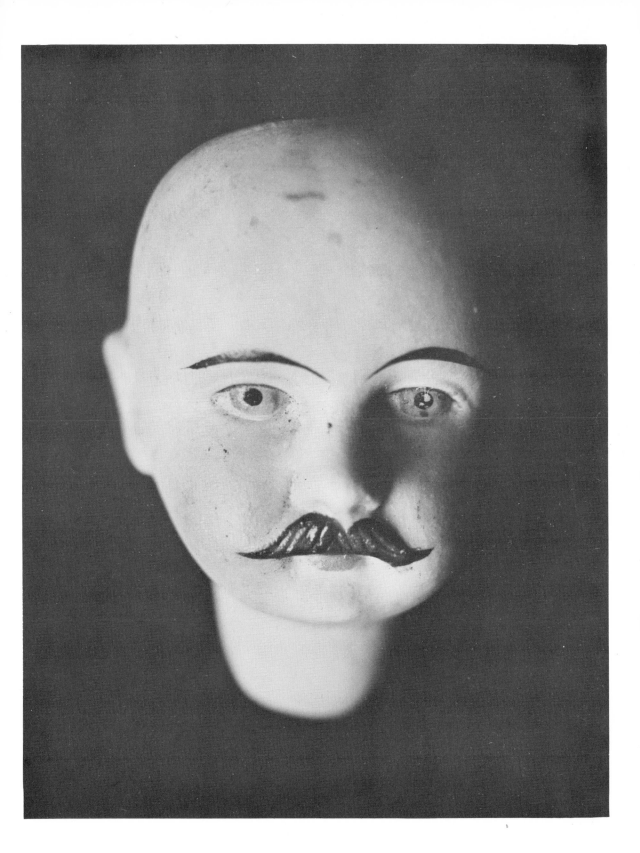

'Pumpkin seed' pocket flask

This pocket flask, protected by a basketwork cover, has a ceramic stopper which is opened and closed by a spring clasp made from iron wire. The flask was made in the early years of the present century and found when a search was made in the garden shed of a derelict Victorian house. Had the flask been thrown into a rubbish dump many years ago only the glass bottle and the ceramic stopper would have survived; wood and metal do not last long in the acid soils within a dump.

Pocket flasks made from glass, earthenware and metal were very popular with Victorian travellers who often faced long and chilling journeys by coach and rail. The bottles usually contained brandy, though earthenware types were also filled with hot water and used as hand warmers. Before 1900 cork stoppers secured to the neck of the bottle by a chain to prevent loss were common.

The use of cane, straw, metal and wood to make coverings for bottles and jars was widespread in those days, especially for bottles which contained valuable liquids such as liqueurs and perfumes. Bottles which had to be transported over long distances by horse-drawn carts only survived the primitive road conditions if they were made from strong glass or if they were enclosed in a protective container.

Miner's lamp

This lamp was my first find on a mining site. I picked it up while exploring a derelict pit-head baths building at a disused colliery in County Durham. Since that day I have found many mining relics around similar sites throughout northern England and I have no doubt that readers who live close to or who visit the old mining areas of Wales, Scotland, Cornwall and elsewhere will also make exciting finds if they search carefully.

Many retired miners still live close to the mine shaft or pit-head in the rows of cottages built by Victorian owners around their mines. These old men know much about the histories of the mines in which they spent their working lives; no opportunity to talk to them should be missed. They usually know the locations of old village dumps and often tell fascinating tales about the dumping of unwanted or obsolete tools and equipment. It is not uncommon to meet a retired miner who still keeps his old tools in a shed at the back of his cottage. He may be prepared to sell them for a small sum if you show interest in such relics.

9 According to the rules

I cannot over-emphasize the importance of obtaining permission for your activities *before* you attempt to recover antiques from the ground on *any* site. 19th-century rubbish dumps, riverside foreshores, derelict houses and all other relic hunting locations you might be drawn to after reading this book are owned by someone; landowners' approval is necessary if you plan to extract objects of value and historical interest from them. It is fortunately the case that such approval is granted far more often than it is withheld. If you keep to the rules which have been evolved by more experienced bottle and relic hunters, and if, whenever possible, you make your request for permission to dig as a member of a bottle collectors' or amateur treasure hunters' club you will rarely meet with refusal.

There are two sets of rules with which you will soon become familiar if you take more than a passing interest in antique and relic hunting using the methods I have outlined. They are the Amateur Treasure Hunters' Code of Conduct and the membership rules of the British Bottle Collectors' Club. Both sets of rules are intended to guide beginners to suitable sites and to ensure that such sites are used in a manner which will not prevent other people enjoying their chosen leisure activities when they wish to use the same piece of land or stretch of riverside.

When inexpensive metal detectors suitable for use by amateur treasure hunters became available in Britain four or five years ago they were widely misused by newcomers to the hobby who were given no advice on their correct use by many retailers who sold them. They were also wantonly misused by amateur archaeologists for purposes other than those for which they were intended. A metal detector is an extremely useful electronic aid to amateur treasure hunting when it is used intelligently on a suitable site. Under ideal conditions a well-designed detector will locate with pin-point accuracy a single coin, a piece of jewellery or any small metal object buried six or eight inches beneath the ground. It is not a magic wand; it cannot guide its user to a site which holds valuables; it does nothing more than signal the presence of a metal object directly beneath its search coil, and it most certainly cannot distinguish between a good amateur treasure hunting site and one on which a detector user will waste his time.

Very few manufacturers and retailers explained these limitations to their customers during the initial wave of popularity which occurred when detectors came on the market. As a result thousands of hopeful fortune hunters who imagined themselves transformed into a combination of King Midas and Cinderella's Godmother were soon wandering across the land, digging holes in municipal golf courses or grubbing about in the flower beds down at the local park.

At the same time a second and smaller group who coveted Celtic gold and Roman silver acquired metal detectors for the purpose of hunting these and other antiquities on archaeological sites. They were not told by detector retailers that on archaeological sites buried metal objects lie too deep in the ground to be located from the surface by electronic instruments. Nor were they told by professional archaeologists that the overwhelming majority of archaeological sites hold few, if any, gold or silver objects. An unsuccessful attempt by professional archaeologists to introduce a law which would have made detector ownership illegal for anyone other than a professional archaeologist simply encouraged the foolish belief that pots of gold could indeed be dug up on the very sites archaeologists were anxious to protect.

Fortunately substantial numbers of intelligent men and women who purchased detectors were quick to realize that detector ownership alone would not make them successful amateur treasure hunters. They joined clubs which were organized by dedicated enthusiasts who understood the hobby and who wished to see it grow. With the help of the Ancient Monuments Secretariat of the Ministry of Works (now the Department of the Environment) these enthusiasts drew up a set of rules to help detector owners become successful amateur treasure hunters and to safeguard ancient sites against vandalism. Responsible detector retailers incorporated these rules into their sales literature and all amateur treasure hunting clubs agreed to abide by them. The rules have since become known as the 'Code of Conduct' and you should be given a copy of them if you purchase a metal detector or when you join an amateur treasure hunting club.

The Code of Conduct

1. Do not interfere with archaeological sites or ancient monuments. Join your local archaeological society if you are interested in ancient history. Genuine amateur treasure hunters concentrate their searches on riversides, beaches, footpaths, commons, houses and gardens. They hunt for lost, hidden or discarded relics dating from the past two or three hundred years.

2. Do not leave a mess on any site you visit. It is perfectly simple to extract a coin or other small objects buried a few inches under the ground without digging a large hole. Use a sharpened trowel or a knife to cut a neat circle, extract the object, replace the soil and grass carefully, and even you will have difficulty in finding the spot again.

3. Help keep Britain tidy—and help yourself. Bottle tops, silver paper and tin cans are the last things you should throw away. You could well be digging them up again next year. Do yourself and the community a favour by taking all rusty junk you find to the nearest litter bin.

4. Do not trespass. Ask permission before venturing onto any private land.

5. Report all unusual historical finds to your local museum and get expert help if you accidentally discover a site of archaeological interest.

6. Learn the Treasure Trove laws and report all finds of gold or silver objects to the police. These laws work to your advantage. If, after a Coroner's inquest, gold or silver objects found by an amateur treasure hunter are declared to be Treasure Trove, the finder must be rewarded to the *full* market value of his find. If the find is not required by a museum it is returned to the finder.

7. Respect the Country Code. Do not leave gates open when crossing fields and do not damage crops or frighten animals.

8. Never miss an opportunity to show and explain your detector to anyone who asks about it. Be friendly. You could pick up some useful clues to a good site.

9. If you meet another detector user introduce yourself. By comparing detector performances and site research notes you will teach yourselves much about the hobby.

114

10. Finally, remember when out with your detector that you are an ambassador for the entire amateur treasure hunting fraternity. Do not give us a bad name.

Bottle collecting also attracted a number of irresponsible diggers when it first achieved widespread popularity a few years ago. Some dug without permission on farmland; others took the view that they could do no harm by digging into local council refuse sites without permission; and I heard of at least one clandestine digger who burrowed into a flood prevention wall on the Thames estuary in the hope of finding Victorian bottles. Fortunately the British Bottle Collectors' Club, whose members include the majority of dump-diggers in this country, was able to act swiftly and decisively against those who behaved in this irresponsible manner. All members are now issued with identity cards which they must sign to indicate acceptance of the Club's rules which are printed on the card. Those rules are:

1. Members must obtain landowners' permission before excavating any site.
2. All finds must be reported to County Secretaries so that local and national records on bottles recovered are kept up-to-date.
3. Every site must be left neat and tidy when an excavation is completed.
4. Failure to observe the above rules renders any member liable to expulsion from the Club.

This talk of rules, regulations and membership cards may sound bureaucratic and irksome to the newcomer eager to get out of doors and dig up his first collectable relic, antique bottle or pot lid; but such disciplines are vital if these hobbies are to survive. In Britain we live on a small and overcrowded island where millions of people pursue a wide variety of outdoor leisure activities and where facilities must often be shared by several groups of pleasure seekers. Imagine the chaos if a party of waterskiers and a sailing club which used the same stretch of water attempted to do so at the same time without benefit of rules and regulations. Our activities—dump-digging, relic hunting, mudlarking, and the rest—are extractive hobbies which, like mining and other extractive industries, could soon mar a beauty spot and spoil someone's pleasure if they were not controlled by self-imposed disciplines.

In practice these regulations will not prevent you making excellent finds. Thousands of amateur treasure hunters have successfully hunted coins, jewellery and other relics with a metal detector in accordance with the Code of Conduct. The finds they have made provide ample proof that the Code actually guides those who abide by it to excellent sites, exciting finds, and a greater appreciation of the pleasures of the hobby.

The British Bottle Collectors' Club has, through its County Secretaries, obtained permission for members to dig on numerous sites throughout the country. Local councils, river authorities, farmers, waste disposal companies and factory owners have all given permission for excavations on their land after reading the Club's rules. Because those members who took part carried out the work in a responsible manner much goodwill now exists between the British Bottle Collectors' Club and many local authorities and large industrial companies on whose land some of the most interesting Victorian dumps are to be found.

Those readers who can find within themselves the patience to persevere when seeking sites on which to dig antiques out of the ground will discover the unforseen pleasures of these hobbies which are unconditionally guaranteed to give years of pleasure and which might even make them rich. With so much to gain I know they will agree the game is worth playing according to the rules.

Books, magazines and clubs

Books

Fletcher, Edward, *Bottle Collecting,* Blandford Press, 1972; *Treasure Hunting for All,* Blandford Press, 1972; *Marble Bottles,* Bottles and Relics Publications, 1974; *Treasure Guide,* Blandford Press, 1975; *Collecting Pot Lids,* Pitman, 1975.

Hindley, Diana and Geoffrey, *Advertising in Victorian England,* Wayland, 1973.

Hume, Ivor Noel, *Treasure in the Thames,* Muller, 1956. (Out of print but worth searching out in libraries.)

Woodhouse, J. C. P., *Victoriana Collectors' Handbook,* Bell, 1972.

Magazines

Bottles and Relics News, G. F. Payne, Editor, 'Greenacres', Church Road, Black Notley, Essex.

Buying Antiques, Embankment Press Ltd, Hutton House, Hutton Street, London EC4Y 8AQ

Clubs

British Bottle Collectors' Club. Initial enquiries regarding membership should be addressed to S. F. Barker, National Secretary, 19 Hambro Avenue, Rayleigh, Essex.

British Amateur Treasure Hunting Club, J. Webb, Secretary, 38 Colet Road, Hutton, Brentwood, Essex.

Index

Nuttall, F., 30

Pegwell Bay, 56
Peters' Mineral Waters, 50
Plumley's Tooth Paste, 95
Plynine Co's Ammonia, 88
Pocket flasks, 109
Pratt, F. and R., 55
Priestley, Joseph, 27
Pub flasks, 34
Pumpkin seeds, 34, 109

Radams, William, 36, 37
Rose, L., 30
Rylands, Ben, 31
Rylands, Dan, 32, 72

'Santa Claus' pipes, 102
Savage's Mineral Waters, 50
Screw stoppers, 33
Sealed bottles, 32, 79
Sillery Champagne, 41
Spong & Co, 48
Stickphast Paste, 49
Stiff, James, 45
Sutcliffe, T., 30
Swanzy's Mineral Waters, 51
Swing stoppers, 34
Sykes, B., 30, 75

Talbot & Co, 72
Tapp, C., 30
Teasdale's Magic Essence, 37
Townsend's Sarsaparilla, 36
Trade Marks Journal, 48, 51, 52
Trotman, F., 30
Tuddingham's Mineral Waters, 50

Vallet, Leon, 30

Warner's Safe Cure, 36, 37, 87
Webb, John, 16
Webb's Indian Tonic, 49
Well's Mineral Waters, 50
Whiskey jars, 82
Wilmer's Mineral Waters, 50
Wood's Areca Nut, 58
Wrought-ironwork, 21